Black College Leadership in PK–12 Education

Black College Leadership in PK–12 Education

Edited by

Ivory A. Toldson

BRILL

LEIDEN | BOSTON

Cover illustration: Image by YANGA; design by Floor Boissevain | Eijgen Stijl (www.eijgenstijl.nl)

All chapters in this book have undergone peer review.

The Library of Congress Cataloging-in-Publication Data is available online at https://catalog.loc.gov

Typeface for the Latin, Greek, and Cyrillic scripts: "Brill". See and download: brill.com/brill-typeface.

ISBN 978-90-04-51758-5 (paperback)
ISBN 978-90-04-51759-2 (hardback)
ISBN 978-90-04-51760-8 (e-book)

Copyright 2022 by Koninklijke Brill NV, Leiden, The Netherlands.
Koninklijke Brill NV incorporates the imprints Brill, Brill Nijhoff, Brill Hotei, Brill Schöningh, Brill Fink, Brill mentis, Vandenhoeck & Ruprecht, Böhlau and V&R unipress.
All rights reserved. No part of this publication may be reproduced, translated, stored in a retrieval system, or transmitted in any form or by any means, electronic, mechanical, photocopying, recording or otherwise, without prior written permission from the publisher. Requests for re-use and/or translations must be addressed to Koninklijke Brill NV via brill.com or copyright.com.

This book is printed on acid-free paper and produced in a sustainable manner.

*To Dr. Ivory Lee Toldson (1943–2012),
my father and former Dean of the School of Education at
Southern University, A&M College*

Contents

Acknowledgments IX
List of Figures and Tables XII
Notes on Contributors XIII

Introduction: Black College Leadership in PK–12 Education 1
    Ivory A. Toldson

1 Strategic Priorities for Historically Black Colleges and Universities with Teacher Preparation Programs 7
    Ivory A. Toldson, Denise Pearson and Nyla Rogers

2 Building Meaningful HBCU and PK–20 Partnerships beyond the Ivory Tower 30
    Allyson L. Watson

3 How Black Colleges Can Recruit, Prepare, and Support Black Male Teachers 45
    Verjanis Peoples and Ivory A. Toldson

4 The Efficacy of Assessment Measures Used for Admission and Certification and Differential Impact on People of Color 57
    Ivan W. Banks

5 Culturally Relevant Pedagogy: Decolonizing the Curriculum and Promoting Educational Equity 78
    Anthony A. Pittman, Dywanna Smith, Delphia S. Smith and Demeturia Kelly

6 HBCUs as a Pathway to Becoming a Scientist: Institutional Characteristics of HBCUs That Are among the Top Baccalaureate Origins of Black Doctorate Recipients in STEM 98
    Ivory A. Toldson, Mercy Mugo, Jennifer Hudson, Mahlet Megra and Cynthia Overton

Acknowledgments

I gratefully acknowledge the people who have directly and indirectly provided me with the support necessary to complete this project.

First, thank you to my wife, Marshella, and my children, Makena and Ivory Kaleb for your enduring love and attention. I'm also thankful for the love and wisdom of my mother Johnita Scott. Thank you to my mother- and father-in-law Janet and Wilbert Atkinson.

Sincere thanks to the National Education Association (NEA) for the technical and financial support for this project. Thank you for Merwyn Scott for understanding the need for HBCU s leadership in PK–12 education, long before the publication of this book. Additional support for this book came from State Higher Education Executive Officers (SHEEO) Association under the leadership of then Vice President, Academic Affairs and Equity Initiatives, Denise Pearson, a longtime HBCU advocate and former HBCU education dean.

Thank you to Jennifer Harris for your conscientious editing and Charles Conteh for dutiful help with organizing tasks. I also thank the leadership at Brill including John Bennett, my publisher, and Jolanda Karada, my production manager.

I am grateful to work with supportive and dynamic people who help me to cultivate ideas through collaborations, dialogue and discourse. This includes the faculty and staff at the Howard University School of Education, the staff of The QEM Network, and *The Journal of Negro Education*; and the National Association for the Advancement of Colored People (NAACP).

Past experiences with national publications, organizations, and foundations also help me to formulate my ideas. For this, I thank: The Thurgood Marshall College Fund under the leadership of Harry L. Williams; UNCF under the leadership of Michael Lomax; the National Science Foundation; The Root; The Congressional Black Caucus Foundation; The White House Initiative on HBCU s; The National Urban League; Alpha Phi Alpha Fraternity; and Sigma Pi Phi Fraternity.

My experiences working with students, teachers and school administrators around the nation, as well as innovative HBCU s help me to gain the perspective necessary to write this book. I've had particularly meaningful experiences working with Broward County Schools, Jefferson County Public Schools, District of Columbia Public Schools, the Virginia Department of Education, and Maryland Commission on Educational Excellence and Innovation (Kirwan Commission).

Thank you for the leadership at Howard University for providing me with the academic environment necessary to produce my scholarship. This includes President Wayne Frederick, Dean Dawn Williams, Chair Kamilah Woodson, and my program director, Angela Ferguson.

Thank you for the leadership at the NAACP for providing me with the network and resolve necessary to activate my work at the grassroots level. This includes President Derrick Johnson, Chief Strategy Officer Yumeka Rushing and Senior Vice President of Strategy and Advancement Jamal Watkins.

Thank you to the many coffee shop baristas and bartenders who accommodated me while I worked on my book from their tables and counters; especially to the teams at Ivy City Smokehouse, The Gathering Spot, Busboys and Poets, and the City Club of Washington DC.

I'm thankful for the guidance of my mentors, my aunt Elsie Scott, Gloria Landson-Billings, Dean Leslie Fenwick, Aaron Stills, Harold Cheatham, A. Wade Boykins, Ronald Braithwaite, Orlando Taylor, Leonard Haynes, Kofi Lomotey, and Ernie Green of the Little Rock Nine.

Finally, thank you to the HBCUs that invited me to your campus to experience your legacy and excellence. I've been to about 45% of all HBCUs, including:

*Alabama A&M University Huntsville, AL
*Alabama State University Montgomery, AL
Allen University Columbia, SC
Benedict College Columbia, SC
*Bennett College for Women Greensboro, NC
Bethune-Cookman University Daytona Beach, FL
*Bowie State University Bowie, MD
Cheyney University of Pennsylvania
*Clark Atlanta University Atlanta, GA
Coppin State University Baltimore, MD
*Dillard University New Orleans, LA
*Fisk University Nashville, TN
*Florida Memorial University Miami Gardens, FL
*Fort Valley State University Fort Valley, GA
Grambling State University Grambling, LA
*Hampton University Hampton, VA
*Howard University Washington, DC
*J.F. Drake State Technical College Huntsville, AL
*Jackson State University Jackson, MS
*LeMoyne-Owen College Memphis, TN

ACKNOWLEDGMENTS

Lincoln University of Pennsylvania
*Meharry Medical College Nashville, TN
*Morehouse College Atlanta, GA
*Morehouse School of Medicine Atlanta, GA
*Morgan State University Baltimore, MD
*North Carolina A&T State University Greensboro, NC
*North Carolina Central University Durham, NC
Oakwood University Huntsville, AL
*Philander Smith College Little Rock, AR
*Prairie View A & M University Prairie View, TX
*Saint Augustine's University Raleigh, NC
Savannah State University Savannah, GA
*Shaw University Raleigh, NC
*Shelton State Community College Tuscaloosa, AL
*Southern University & A&M College Baton Rouge, LA
Southern University at New Orleans New Orleans, LA
*Spelman College Atlanta, GA
*Stillman College Tuscaloosa, AL
*Tennessee State University Nashville, TN
*Texas Southern University Houston, TX
*University of Arkansas at Pine Bluff Pine Bluff, AR
*University of the District of Columbia
*Virginia State University Petersburg, VA
*Xavier University of Louisiana New Orleans, LA

*Delivered a speech

Figures and Tables

Figures

1.1 A model illustrating the relationship between state government and the ability of HBCUs to implement robust teacher preparation programs that can diversify the teacher workforce with qualified teachers that serve the unique needs of various school districts.   16

6.1 A Du Boisian adaptation of the three isomorphic pressures (DiMaggio & Powell, 1983) that influence institutional policies and practices at HBCUs in ways that can be inconsistent with their mission to serve underserved students.   104

6.2 Anchor scoring system and cutoff score for emerging institutions.   115

Tables

1.1 Racial disparities in discipline occurring in districts that are adjacent to HBCUs.   9

1.2 Racial disparities in college preparation occurring in school districts that are adjacent to HBCUs.   12

1.3 Racial disparities in resource allocation occurring in school districts that are adjacent to HBCUs.   15

6.1 Basic characteristics of institutions.   105

6.2 Categories and source variables used to characterize institutions.   106

6.3 Summary statistics of assessed continuous variables for analysis.   108

6.4 Summary statistics of assessed categorical variables for analysis.   112

6.5 List of emerging institutions identified.   116

Notes on Contributors

Ivan W. Banks
is the vice-chair on the Board of Directors for the Society for College and University Planning (SCUP), the advisory board of the Region 7 Comprehensive Center; and researcher and advisor for the National Institutes for Underserved Students. In 2020, Banks retired as a professor from Alcorn State University in Mississippi where he also served as dean of the School of Education and Psychology, executive director of the Vicksburg Expansion Campus, director of online education, and associate provost. In New Jersey, Banks was appointed by the commissioner of education to serve on the Higher Education Taskforce that was charged with making recommendations for policies and procedures to govern processes for the preparation of teachers and other professional school personnel. Banks completed his bachelor's degree in history and sociology with an Ohio teacher's certification at Case Western Reserve University; a master's degree in education (economics) at John Carroll University, and a doctorate of education in instructional design and educational technology at the University of Kentucky.

Jennifer Hudson
is a Senior Researcher in the Human Services program at American Institutes for Research (AIR). Here, Dr. Hudson manages multiple education research projects focused on STEM equity across public schools and within postsecondary education. Previously, Dr. Hudson was Chair of the Human Subject Research Review Committee (HSRRC) for the Virginia Department of Corrections and Annie E. Casey Leaders in Equitable Evaluation and Diversity (LEEAD) Fellow. She is the recent recipient of AIR's 2021 Equity Initiative "Scholars and Leaders" grant award to investigate advanced course availability and access in public secondary schools.

Demeturia Kelly
is the educational technologist in the School of Education at Claflin University. While at Claflin University, Mr. Kelly has served as a Mentor and then Director of Project Pipeline Repair (PPR): is a State Higher Education Executive Officers (SHEEO) initiative to increase the representation of minority males in the teaching profession and assist states in their efforts to stem teacher shortages. Through this program, Mr. Kelly and CUSOE worked with 10 minority male high school juniors and seniors that planned to enroll in an Educator Preparation Program (EPP) at an HBCU after completing high school in hopes of becoming a teacher. Before becoming a teacher, Mr. Kelly worked in the Department of

Education at South Carolina State University as a Technology Specialist where he assisted the Department's Assessment Coordinator with data related to accreditation.

Mahlet Megra
(MS, PMP) is a senior survey methodologist at the American Institutes for Research (AIR). She works on various data collection and analyses projects. She develops analyses plans, conducts quantitative analyses, provides methodological expertise, and writes technical reports for federal agencies such as the National Center for Education Statistics and the Institute of Museums and Library Services. She graduated with a Master's in Survey Methodology from the Joint Program in Survey Methodology at the University of Maryland.

Mercy Mugo
is the executive director at the Quality Education for Minorities (QEM) Network. Dr. Mugo has almost 10 years of experience in the design and implementation of capacity building and educational research projects focused on advancing the academic and research goals of students and faculty at minority-serving institutions (MSIs). Her work is centered on efforts to broaden the participation of groups historically underrepresented in science, technology, engineering, and mathematic (STEM) education and careers. She is PI on several major grants focused on combating disparities in STEM educational and career outcomes among underrepresented minorities. She has co-authored several articles about research productivity at Historically Black Colleges and Universities (HBCUs). She holds a BA in Education from the University of Nairobi, Kenya, and an MA and PhD in Psychometrics from Morgan State University.

Cynthia Overton
is the senior director of Tech Workplace Initiatives at the Kapor Center. Here, Dr. Overton leads a certificate program focused on advancing diversity and inclusion in the tech industry. She also organizes Diversity Advocates, a professional learning community for diversity and inclusion professionals in tech, and Our Collective, an online community of tech professionals working to advance inclusion for people of color in tech through employee resource groups. When she's not working, Cynthia enjoys consuming content, writing, or speaking about Web3 and what this new iteration of the internet will mean for historically excluded populations.

Denise Pearson
is the vice-chancellor and Chief Diversity, Equity, and Inclusion Officer for Pennsylvania's State System of Higher Education. Dr. Pearson has more than 25

years of experience in higher education including academic affairs, policy analysis, and teacher preparation. Dr. Pearson is an author and nationally sought-after speaker, elevating the critical role of system-level strategic planning, HBCUs and educational equity, inclusive excellence, and teacher diversity.

Verjanis Peoples
is the director of the School of Education at Southern University and A&M College, professor of education, and vice-president of the Peoples Advanced Consulting Group, in Baton Rouge, LA. Dr. Peoples also serves as director of the nationally recognized program, Project Pipeline Repair: Restoring Minority Male Participation and Persistence in Educator Preparation Programs. The purpose of this State Higher Education Executive Officers (SHEEO) initiative, is to increase the representation of minority males in the teaching profession and assist the state in efforts to increase the number of STEM teachers. Dr. Peoples served as Executive Vice Chancellor for Academic Affairs at Southern University and A&M College, where she was successful in propelling the university to higher grounds in academia and student success programs.

Anthony A. Pittman
is the dean of the School of Education and a professor at Claflin University. He maintains more than twenty-plus years of experience in the education profession and his teaching career has spanned the entire gamut of all instructional levels from early childhood education up through adult and continuing education. He has presented at numerous professional conferences, drawing attention to such topics as African American Males in Higher Education; Manhood, Masculinity, and the Education of African American Males; Bilingual Education; and Developing and Implementing Standards for Social Justice in Education. His book, *Whited Out: Unique Perspective on Black Identity and Honors Achievement*, has provided deep insight into the topic of equal access to quality educational programs, especially for those from underrepresented populations.

Nyla Rogers
is a research associate at Quality Education for Minorities Network and a doctoral student at Howard University. Mrs. Rogers conducts research in areas around health and wellness for people of color. Mrs. Rogers has conducted workshops at numerous conferences across the nation intending to elevate Black consciousness. She has authored and contributed to research papers in areas such as the impact of racial discrimination and the importance of HBCUs. Other research interests include spirituality, grief, interpersonal relationships (romantic and familial), and resiliency in Black marriage.

Delphia S. Smith

is an assistant professor, faculty advisor, and curriculum committee chair in the School of Education at Claflin University. She serves as Curriculum Committee Chair in the School of Education and Faculty Advisor for the School of Education Student Advisory Council. Before entering the academy, Dr. Smith served as an elementary educator for over 11 years in the United States and her home country, the Bahamas. A lover of reading and writing, Dr. Smith has co-authored several children's books that focus on areas such as race, diversity, and the importance of hard work and dedication.

Dywanna Smith

is an assistant professor, middle-level program coordinator, and advisement ambassador for the School of Education at Claflin University.

Ivory A. Toldson

is the national director of Education Innovation and Research for the NAACP, professor of counseling psychology at Howard University and editor-in-chief of *The Journal of Negro Education*. Toldson is ranked among the nation's top education professors as a member of Education Week's Edu-Scholar Public Influence Rankings. Toldson was appointed by President Barack Obama to devise national strategies to sustain and expand federal support to HBCUs as the executive director of the White House Initiative on Historically Black Colleges and Universities (WHIHBCUs). Toldson has served as principal investigator of 12 National Science Foundation and NASA awards, totaling more than $7 million, to support capacity building efforts for STEM programs at HBCUs and other Minority Serving Institutions.

Allyson L. Watson

is the dean of the College of Education at the Florida Agricultural and Mechanical University. Dr. Watson has focused her research on innovation in education, STEM in urban education, women and faculty of color in higher education, and urban school and university partnerships. She is a full professor and tenured graduate faculty with substantial teaching and research experience in educational research, advanced educational measurements and statistics, public school relations, and instructional strategies. Dr. Watson spent over 20 years teaching and leading in Tulsa, Oklahoma which shaped her passion for encouraging teachers to include accurate history within culturally responsive pedagogy.

INTRODUCTION

Black College Leadership in PK–12 Education

Ivory A. Toldson

Black colleges, also known as historically Black colleges and universities (HBCUs), have played a prominent role in advancing Black educational progress in the United States and abroad. As defined in the *Higher Education Act* of 1965, HBCUs are Black colleges and universities that gained accreditation before 1964 and whose primary responsibility was, and still is, educating Americans of Black African ancestry (Preston & Palmer, 2018). The first HBCU was Cheyney University, founded in 1837 (Crewe, 2017), followed by Lincoln University (1854) and Wilberforce University (1856). At present, the number of HBCUs slightly exceeds one hundred, which accounts for nearly 3% of post-secondary schools (Preston & Palmer, 2018).

Since their foundation, HBCUs have experienced various levels of demand and have served different purposes depending on the prevailing social issues in the nation. However, an undoubted fact about HBCUs is that they have always pursued the noble mission of making the lives of Black Americans richer in terms of the opportunities they received and the knowledge they gained. This book explores the role of HBCUs in creating a more equitable educational environment for Black students and advancing American society through inclusive pre-kindergarten through twelfth grade (PK–12) education.

1   Black College Leadership in Education during Our Nation's Infancy

The first HBCUs were established before the first anniversary of the United States' founding, creating opportunities for newly emancipated Black people. In 1862, the first *Morrill Land Grant Act* (Harper, Patton, & Wooden, 2009) helped to start the educational movement in mechanical arts and agriculture. The second *Morrill Act* of 1890 endowed equal funds for Black universities and colleges in seventeen states. Although the Act had a noble purpose, educational facilities did not receive the promised funding. As a result, instead of focusing on agricultural and mechanical arts, many HBCUs concentrated on training Black students to become teachers, and thus more qualified high school educators entered the Black community. As a result, more African American parents sent their children to school, nurturing growth in subsequent student generations (Craig, 1992).

Despite some shortcomings, the *Morrill Acts* presented a significant opportunity to cultivate Black education. About 90% of African Americans who received a university degree in the first decades of the 1900s were graduates of HBCUs. Despite the poor financial conditions of HBCUs prior to the 1900s, these institutions served to enhance the quality of life for Black people and other underserved populations. The prevailing ideology of the 1862–1900 period was "racial uplift" (Crewe, 2017, p. 361). This suggested that African Americans were accountable for their race's welfare, which encouraged young people to use their education as a tool against attempts to limit their civil and political rights.

The first HBCUs were more than merely educational establishments: They were also places that aimed to bolster the African American community through intellectual development. For example, the mission of Morehouse College, founded in 1867, was to resist Jim Crow laws aimed at discriminating against Black people and promoting segregation (Jensen, 2017). The educational process at the college had a profound effect on developing Black religious and educational opportunities. Three decades before Morehouse College was established, Cheyney University opened, when about one fifth of African Americans were illiterate (Crewe, 2017). Cheyney University became the most significant driving force in fostering a new life position for post-abolitionist Black citizens in the reconstruction era.

Mission statements of the first HBCUs founded between 1865 and 1869 included such aspects as providing high-quality education, cultivating creativity and social responsibility, and developing a society in which all citizens could have their needs satisfied. Further, improving societal attitudes toward the race question was not only an institutional purpose but also a personal one (Crewe, 2017). Faculty members and students realized that the future of their race depended on their efforts. The missions of the first universities and colleges incorporated anti-discrimination efforts as well as establishing equal opportunities for the future.

2   Black College Leadership in Education and the Fight for Civil Rights

From the 1900s to 1940s, there was a heightened realization of Black people's cultural contribution to the nation's development. Historically Black fraternities and sororities formed, and HBCU leadership transitioned from white charities to Black Americans. A renaissance of African American scholarship emerged at HBCUs during this period, and HBCUs started evolving into entities that were fertile for civil rights movements.

African Americans started movements for self-assertion and resistance (Dodson, 2016), as the New Negro movement paved the way for the civil rights movement, which inspired Black people to fight for equality. HBCUs played a leading role in the fight for civil rights, since their students became important participants within these movements (Barrett, 2017). HBCU graduates created a new generation of African American people who spared no effort to validate their identity as human beings and prove that they could do much more than the United States government expected of them (Dodson, 2016).

During this time, the founding of the Niagara movement led to the creation of the National Association for the Advancement of Colored People in 1908. The NAACP made contributions to education and the arts through *The Crisis*. The magazine, spearheaded by W. E. B. Du Bois, incorporated the first periodical for Black youth in America called *The Brownies' Book*. It was distributed on Black college campuses during the Harlem Renaissance and focused on political, social, economic, educational, moral, and ethical issues facing Black children and youth as well as the rise of Black colleges.

Black colleges were "ready-made" hubs for activism and involvement with local NAACP chapters (Barrett, 2017). Some of the earliest HBCU activism inspired by NAACP literature took place at Fisk University, Morgan State University, and Howard University. Influenced by writings in *The Crisis* and similar periodicals, students at HBCUs rejected the ideas of white philanthropists having control over the conditions of Black colleges, and in 1925 Fisk University students protested poor campus conditions (Rogers, 2009).

Protests began in February and lasted until the resignation of President Fayette Avery McKenzie two months later. The Fisk strike influenced students on other HBCU campuses to assert their existence as men and women who did not need white paternalism on or off campus (Lamon, 1974). Similar protests ensued through the 1920s to 1940s at Morgan State University and Howard University. In 1939, many of Morgan State students became members of the NAACP and participated in the first national youth conference (Barrett, 2017). Many of these young people were also representatives at the City-Wide Young People's Forum, which originated in 1931.

Apart from the NAACP (founded in 1909), such organizations as the National Association of Colored Women (1895), the National Urban League (1910), and the Association for the Study of Negro Life and History (1915) appeared. The *Plessy v. Ferguson* case, the main impetus for the development of these organizations, made African Americans rise in defense of their race to eliminate the unfair effects of segregation. Within ten years following *Plessy v. Ferguson*, HBCUs and Black organizations coalesced into a national Black movement that aimed to resist post-reconstruction terrorism. Both local and national associations created by African Americans from the 1900s until the 1940s helped to bolster the rights and social position of Black people (Dodson, 2016).

3   Black College Leadership in Dismantling Educational Apartheid in America

HBCUs played a crucial role in the civil rights movement of the 1950s and 1960s. HBCUs provided intellectual leadership, foot soldiers, and secure places to meet and plan (Williamson, 2004). During *Brown v. Board of Education*, HBCUs served as a "repository of hope" for universal education of every individual (Jean-Marie, 2006, p. 87). The participation of HBCU students in the civil rights movement nurtured the educational, civic engagement, and spiritual goals of African American youth.

HBCUs also provided the intellectual prowess needed to build a case against educational apartheid. Nearly eighty years ago, Drs. Kenneth and Mamie Clark used innovative research to help dismantle the legal justification for segregation in schools. Both Dr. Kenneth Clark and Dr. Mamie Clark were HBCU educated. Dr. Kenneth Clark started the psychology department at the Hampton Institute (now Hampton University). In coordination with lawyers based at the Howard University School of Law, Drs. Kenneth and Mamie Clark completed the seminal "doll experiments," which they published in the *Journal of Negro Education*, an HBCU-based publication started by Howard University School of Education's dean, Charles Henry Thompson (Clark & Clark, 1950).

Clark and Clark's (1950) research studies were transdisciplinary, connecting psychology, law, and education, and they used a rigorous scientific methodology that was novel at the time. Moreover, the research was conceived and interpreted from a Black perspective, enabled through publication in a Black-operated peer-refereed research journal. Rather than perpetuating deficit narratives that focused on disfunctions of Black identity, the studies interrogated institutional racism. A Black child identifying with a white doll was not positioned as the central issue – rather, it was a by-product of the true central issue – legal segregation. This audaciously Black research enterprise compelled the US Supreme Court to overturn *Plessy v. Fergurson* in *Brown v. Board of Education*, the landmark decision that ruled segregation in public schools to be unconstitutional (Carter, 2007).

4   Black College Leadership in PK–12 Education

Educational equity, inclusion, belonging, and justice are widely considered to be the most important civil rights challenges of the 21st century. Many HBCUs began in the 1800s as institutions to prepare Black teachers to teach in segregated America. Although their focus has expanded since their critical beginnings, HBCUs remain significant producers of African American teachers. Today, as the United States grapples with educational disparities, lack of diversity among education professionals, systemic racism, and the recent politically inspired assaults on critical race theory, we need HBCU leadership in PK–12 education more than ever.

Black College Leadership in PK–12 Education amplifies the research and perspectives of HBCU leaders, including four HBCU education deans, on how HBCUs help school districts optimize education for Black preschool, elementary, and secondary students. Specific topics include HBCU teacher preparation, building HBCU and PK–12 partnerships, culturally responsive teaching, inclusive assessment practices, and HBCU leadership in STEM education. This book is ideal for schoolteachers and administrators who want to use HBCUs as a resource to improve education, as well as HBCU leaders who want to work more effectively with local school districts.

References

Barrett, S. R. (2017). *"We bring thee our laurels whatever they may be": A concise history of Morgan State College student-led protest.* Morgan State University Digital Dissertations.

Carter, R. (2007). Brown's legacy: Fulfilling the promise of equal education. *Journal of Negro Education, 76*(3), 240–249. www.jstor.org/stable/40034568

Clark, K., & Clark, M. (1950). Emotional factors in racial identification and preference in negro children. *Journal of Negro Education, 19*(3), 341–350. doi:10.2307/2966491

Craig, L. A. (1992). "Raising among themselves": Black educational advancement and the Morrill Act of 1890. *Agriculture and Human Values, 9*(1), 31–37.

Crewe, S. E. (2017). Education with intent – the HBCU experience. *Journal of Human Behavior in the Social Environment, 27*(5), 360–366. doi:10.1080/10911359.2017.1318622

Dodson, H. (2016). Howard University, the New Negro movement, and the making of African American visual arts in Washington, DC: Part 1. *Callaloo, 39*(5), 983–998. doi:10.1353/cal.2016.0138

Harper, S. R., Patton, L. D., & Wooden, O. A. (2009). Access and equity for African American students in higher education: A critical race historical analysis of policy efforts. *Journal of Higher Education, 80*(4), 389–414.

Jean-Marie, G. (2006). Welcoming the unwelcome: A social justice imperative of African-American female leaders at historically black colleges and universities. *Educational Foundations, 20*(1), 85–104.

Jensen, K. E. (2017). Pedagogical personalism at Morehouse College. *Studies in Philosophy and Education, 36*(2), 147–165.

Lamon, L. C. (1974). The Black community in Nashville and the Fisk University student strike of 1924–1935. *Journal of Southern History, 40*, 225–244.

Preston, D. C., & Palmer, R. T. (2018). When relevance is no longer the question. *Journal of Black Studies, 49*(8), 782–800. https://www.jstor.org/stable/26574595

Rogers, I. H. (2009). Remembering the Black campus movement: An oral history interview with James P. Garrett. *Journal of Pan African Studies, 2*(10), 30–41.

Williamson, J. A. (2004). "This has been quite a year for heads falling": Institutional autonomy in the Civil Rights era. *History of Education Quarterly, 44*(04), 554–576. doi:10.1111/j.1748-5959.2004.tb00020.x

CHAPTER 1

Strategic Priorities for Historically Black Colleges and Universities with Teacher Preparation Programs

Ivory A. Toldson, Denise Pearson and Nyla Rogers

Racial disparities prevail across all aspects of public school education, affecting disciplinary measures, academic achievement, college readiness, and resource allocation. Educational equity is widely considered the civil rights challenge of the 21st century. Many historically Black colleges and universities (HBCU s) began as institutions to prepare teachers to teach in segregated America. Although their focus has expanded since their critical beginnings, they remain significant producers of the country's educators of color – particularly African American teachers. For this chapter, we surveyed extant research, data, and four HBCU schools of education to help state higher education executives and nongovernmental organizations understand what drives successful teacher preparation at HBCU s.

Increasing the number and capacity of underrepresented minority teachers from HBCU s will diversify the teacher workforce, which can contribute to America's global competitiveness. The millennial population, now larger than the baby boomers, is the most racially diverse adult population in US history. By the mid-2040s, the majority of the US population will be people of color. For the United States to remain globally competitive, we must widen the teacher pipeline and ensure broad participation by Americans of all races. HBCU s are important incubators of teachers of color – however, institutional challenges can undermine HBCU s' best efforts to recruit, retain, and prepare students of color to become teachers.

1   Racial Disparities within Public School Districts

The Department of Education's Civil Rights Data Collection suggests that opportunity gaps that exist between Black and white students across the country center around three key areas: (1) schools discipline Black students more harshly by suspending them for behaviors (e.g., tardiness) that rarely result in suspensions among white students; (2) schools routinely offer Black students a less rigorous curriculum that omits classes required for college admission; and (3) Black students are the most likely to attend school in segregated learning environments that have fewer resources to educate their students. This section reviews the literature on these aspects of racial disparities in school and analyzes secondary data to determine if these issues occur in HBCU-adjacent school districts.

1.1 Discipline

Racial disparities in discipline are acute in US public schools. Morris and Perry (2016) note that racial disparities in adulthood, including in health, employment, and incarceration, are connected to inequalities in academic achievement, which arise from unfairly distributed disciplinary measures. Carter, Skiba, Arredondo, and Pollock (2016) argue that despite numerous attempts to counteract bias and stereotypes at schools, institutional prejudice persists. Due to sustained processes of colorblindness, microaggressions, and implicit bias, African American students nationwide suffer from unfair treatment and more severe disciplinary measures than white students. The first step in eliminating racial inequalities in discipline is recognizing their existence.

Statistics on discipline available from a nationwide report are alarming. In most states, Black students are suspended between three and six times more than white students (Groeger, Waldman, & Eads, 2018). Scholars investigating disparities in school discipline note a variety of negative consequences. Skiba, Arredondo, and Rausch (2014) report that persistent racial disparities in suspensions lead to low graduation rates and more frequent involvement in the criminal justice system. The situation becomes further aggravated by gender disparities within the racial groups. Notably, the most vulnerable group is Black male students.

Researchers have concluded that racial inequality in discipline did not emerge recently but has been evolving for centuries due to many historical events and processes. Carter et al. (2016) assert that slavery, forced migration, and other factors that promoted unfair treatment of Black people created social and economic discrimination. Racial disparities are hard to overcome because of the unwillingness of many Americans to acknowledge their existence. Hence, to eliminate the prevalence of discipline inequalities, society in general, and the system of education specifically, must first engage in a conversation about the problem.

1.2 Racial Disparities in Discipline Occurring in Districts That Are Adjacent to HBCUs

Table 1.1 displays indicators of racial disparities in discipline in nine school districts that are adjacent to four HBCUs. All HBCU-adjacent school districts

TABLE 1.1 Racial disparities in discipline occurring in districts that are adjacent to HBCUs

HBCU	Adjacent school district	Total enrollment	% Black	Total N out-of-school suspensions	% Black out-of-school suspensions	Total N expulsions	% Black expulsions	Total N students referred to law enforcement
Alcorn State University	Watson Chapel School District	2,603	74.8%	285	83.2%	18	100%	7
	Pine Bluff School District	1,485	98.8%	248	95.2%	0	0%	60
University of Arkansas at Pine Bluff	Claiborne County School District	4,507	95.6%	518	99.2%	9	100%	100
	Dollarway School District	1,295	92.5%	448	95.1%	6	100%	0
Claflin University	Orangeburg Consolidated School District 3	2,883	87.2%	1,006	90%	10	100%	4
	Orangeburg Consolidated School District 4	3,776	45.5%	804	59.3%	76	55.3%	15
	Orangeburg Consolidated School District 5	6,629	87.1%	1,355	92.3%	27	100%	0
Southern University and A & M College	East Baton Rouge Parish	42,609	78.1%	599	94.7%	737	90.8%	109
	West Baton Rouge Parish	3,884	51.9%	62	77.4%	120	79.2%	0

Note: Data from the U.S. Department of Education Civil Rights Data Collection (CRDC), which collects and reports data on key education and civil rights issues in public schools. (https://ocrdata.ed.gov/) (Survey Year: 2015)

except for one are majority Black school districts, ranging from 98.8% to 51.9%. With respect to out-of-school suspensions, all districts except one suspend Black students at a rate that is disproportionally higher than their representation in the student body. Black students in many of this these districts also experience expulsions and school-based arrest. East Baton Rouge Parish, which is the largest HBCU-adjacent school district that we surveyed, had the largest total number of school-based arrests and expulsions, with 737. Interestingly, West Baton Rouge Parish, a district of 3,884, expelled 120 students. By comparison, Orangeburg Consolidated School District 5, a district of 6,629 students, expelled 27.

1.3 *Academic Achievement and College Preparation*

According to statistical data, the rate of academic opportunity is higher among white students than among non-white students. For instance, white learners are 1.8 times more likely than African Americans to be in advanced-placement classes (Groeger et al., 2018). Furthermore, as Grissom and Redding (2016) note, high-achieving Black students are underrepresented in gifted programs. As the US Department of Education reports, in 2009, Black students constituted 16.7% of the general student population, but only 9.8% of Black students participated in gifted programs.

The underrepresentation of African American students in gifted programs, in addition to dual credit opportunities, corresponds with lower achievement among this learner group. However, the unfair distribution of students in gifted programs occurs because of other negative issues. For instance, Black students' families are less likely than white families to obtain information about the processes to be identified for gifted programs. Further, African American families rarely have access to a private psychologist or some other specialist who could assess their child's abilities. Data available on elementary school students indicates that only 83% of Black children attend schools with gifted programs, in contrast to 91% of Asians and 90% of whites (Grissom & Redding, 2016). At the school level, African American learners are more likely to remain unnoticed in this regard compared to white students. Teachers are among the core determinants of selecting children to participate in gifted programs. Educators make referrals, thus playing "a gatekeeping role" in student allocation to gifted programs (Grissom & Redding, 2016, p. 1).

Academic achievement is the factor that predicts students' ability to enter a college upon graduation. As Bryant (2015) remarks, attaining a college degree is fundamental to eliminating poverty and closing the wealth gap between white and Black people living in the US. In modern society, the acquisition of postsecondary education has become a prerequisite for success in the job market. For 2020, it has been estimated that nearly 66% of jobs required a college degree, 30% of them calling for at least a bachelor's degree (Bryant, 2015). Thus, under these circumstances, more young people should complete a college degree to be able to find a well-paying job. Still, the majority of Black students leave high school without proper preparation to enter a college.

The insufficient readiness to obtain college education by African American students is one of the burdens of the modern education system. What is more, due to demographic shifts, the majority of US students are non-white (Bryant, 2015). Therefore, not preparing non-white students for college will have negative consequences for the nation's economy and labor market. It is common practice to attribute Black students' poor performance in school to family issues and cultural and environmental divergence. However, a far more important factor – which, unfortunately, does not receive substantial attention – is the deficiencies in school systems (Bryant, 2015). It is necessary to analyze these flaws to find out how the US system of education might remedy them.

Scholars have identified three principal educational barriers that play a crucial role in students' readiness to enter college: lack of access to preparatory courses, school counselors, and experienced educators (Bryant, 2015). The first aspect concerns the need for rigorous courses where students could improve their content knowledge and enrich their higher-order thinking skills. Participation in such courses can enhance students' college readiness. However, minority students do not have enough access to these opportunities. The second aspect is the role of school counselors, who constitute an important advantage for those seeking college education. School counselors serve as learners' advocates and encourage students to pursue their cherished academic dreams. Nonetheless, as Bryant (2015) reports, school counselors frequently discourage Black students from pursuing a college degree by demonstrating no interest or belief in their knowledge and skills.

Experienced teachers can promote students' knowledge and college readiness. African American students often do not have access to schools with teachers who are invested in inculcating knowledge and establishing positive relationships with Black students. In addition, most Black students are first-generation college students (Black, Cortes, & Lincove, 2015; Bryant, 2015). To increase college readiness among African American students, it is necessary to alter the system of education by providing Black students with access to schools with experienced teachers and knowledgeable counselors.

1.4 Racial Disparities in College Readiness Occurring in Districts That Are Adjacent to HBCUs

Table 1.2 displays indicators of the racial disparities that exist with college preparation in nine school districts that are adjacent to four HBCUs. With respect to participation in gifted programs, all districts except three enroll

TABLE 1.2 Racial disparities in college preparation occurring in school districts that are adjacent to HBCUs

HBCU	Adjacent school district	Total enrollment	% Black	% Black in gifted & talented	Total N students in calculus	Total black students in calculus	% Black in calculus	Total N students in physics	Total black students in physics	% Black in physics
Alcorn State University	Watson Chapel School District	2,603	74.8%	55.2%	*	*	*	19	13	68.4%
	Claiborne Country School District	1,485	98.8%	100%	19	19	100%	19	19	100%
University of Arkansas at Pine Bluff	Pine Bluff School District	4,507	95.6%	96.3%	25	25	100%	25	25	100%
	Dollarway School District	1,295	92.5%	91.9%	*	*	*	21	19	90.5%
Claflin University	Orangeburg Consolidated School District 3	2,883	87.2%	74.5%	13	13	100%	30	28	93.3%
	Orangeburg Consolidated School District 3	3,766	45.5%	20.1%	14	4	28.6%	54	28	51.9%
	Orangeburg Consolidated School District 3	6,629	87.1%	88.2%	34	26	76.5%	102	81	79.4%
Southern University and A & M College	East Baton Rouge Parish	42,609	78.1%	48.2%	852	485	56.9%	913	690	75.6%
	West Baton Rouge Parish	3,884	51.9%	36.2%	24	4	16.7%	11	4	36.44%

Note: Data from the U.S. Department of Education Civil Rights Data Collection (CRDC), which collects and reports data on key education and civil right issues in public schools. (https://ocrdata.ed.gov/) (Survey Year: 2015)
*Values not reported.

Black students at a rate that is disproportionally lower than their representation in the student body. Black students in many of these districts also experience lower than expected enrollment in calculus and physics. East Baton Rouge Parish, which is the largest HBCU-adjacent school district that we surveyed, had the worst inequities. This district is 78% Black, yet gifted programs are only 48% Black and calculus enrollment is only 56.9% Black. A Black student in East Baton Rouge is more likely to be expelled than to take Calculus.

1.5 Resource Allocation and School Segregation

Racial segregation and student achievement are closely linked (Reardon, 2016). African American students, as well as other minority groups, frequently become isolated in schools where socioeconomic and racial segregation prevail. Over 80% of Black students attend majority-minority schools, with more than 60% of their classmates living in low-income families (Flashman, 2014). Studies have associated segregation patterns with the achievement gap. In the past, scholars considered school segregation and resource allocation intertwined (Gamoran & An, 2016), finding that schools attended by African American students did not receive adequate resources.

The politics of school segregation presuppose that students belonging to minority ethnic groups attend certain types of schools that typically do not attract socially and economically advantaged populations. According to Munk, McMillan, and Lewis (2014), many people consider low-income and minority learners as those with poor learning outcomes. Researchers distinguish between several problems related to school segregation. First, schools with many Black students must deal with more learner needs for emotional, educational, medical, and physical support. Second, such schools often do not have enough noncommercial resources. Third, these schools also have difficulty hiring and retaining qualified teachers, or there may be disunity between the dominant school culture and those of minority students (Munk et al., 2014). Furthermore, segregated schools may suffer from low student and teacher engagement levels.

Since segregation has a direct effect on students' achievement, it is vital to analyze the ways in which this negative phenomenon occurs and the reasons for its emergence. Reardon (2016) offers an elaborate classification of school segregation types: school and residential segregation, between-school and between-district discrepancies, and students' exposure to poor neighbors or classmates. There are two main ways of measuring segregation: exposure and unevenness. Exposure (or isolation) measures indicate the average socioeconomic or racial structure of the schools or neighborhoods of students. For instance, the median rate of Black students in an African American child's school or neighborhood represents the measure of racial isolation. Meanwhile, the unevenness measure explains the disparity in the median socioeconomic or racial school arrangement between students with different racial backgrounds (Reardon, 2016). Therefore, while exposure measures characterize the context of students of a particular race, unevenness measures express the variation in average circumstances between the two racial groups. Simply put, unevenness measures indicate the differences in exposure measures.

Segregation is partially responsible for the achievement gap between white and Black students. According to Gamoran and An (2016), the No Child Left Behind project, which was initiated to set guidelines for performance, revealed dramatic statistics regarding many schools and that a growing number of them could not meet the project's standard. One of the principal reasons for such failure was that schools with a high degree of minority students demonstrated low scores. It thus demonstrated that segregation has a negative effect on Black students' achievement. To eliminate the prevalence of such outcomes, it is necessary to reduce the level of school segregation in the US.

1.6   Racial Disparities in Resource Allocation in Districts That Are Adjacent to HBCUs

Table 1.3 displays indicators of racial disparities in resource allocation in nine school districts that are adjacent to four HBCUs. All districts surveyed had an adequate number of full-time teachers to accommodate the size of the district. However, issues noted in previous sections suggests that many teachers, who may have the proper licensing and certification requirements and are teaching a manageable number of students, are not adequately prepared to mitigate racial disparities. In addition, all districts have a small number of counselors, which reduces opportunities for meaningful engagement with students to adequately prepare them for postsecondary success.

2   Conversations with HBCU School of Education Deans

2.1   Theory of Change

This study was grounded in institutional theory, a sociological framework that examines the influence of institutional contexts on the structures of organizations (Meyer & Rowan, 1977; Tolbert & Zucker, 1996), as well as critical race theory. For this book, we were interested in the institutional context of HBCU policies and programs, as these can serve as powerful traditions to influence students' motivation and desire to achieve against the backdrop of racial inequities in PK–12 education. Theoretically, HBCUs have formal organizational structures with both symbolic and action-generating aspects. The symbolic aspects (e.g., mission and executive leadership) influence HBCUs' structures and practices and are motivated by the need for legitimacy and survival.

TABLE 1.3 Racial disparities in resource allocation occurring in school districts that are adjacent to HBCUs

HBCU	Adjacent school district	Total enrollment	Total teachers (FTE)	Total counselors (FTE)	% Teachers meeting all state licensing and certification requirements (FTE)	% Teachers in 1st year of teaching (FTE)	Teachers absent >10 days of the school year (FTE)	Students to teachers (FTE) ratio
Alcorn State University	Watson Chapel School District	2,603	169	8	99.4	1.8	84	15:1
	Claiborne County School District	1,485	97	4	96.9	5.2	59	15:1
University of Arkansas at Pine Bluff	Pine Bluff School District	4,507	331	12	99.4	5.4	50	14:1
	Dollarway School District	1,295	101	5	76.9	12.8	10	13:1
Claflin University	Orangeburg Consolidated School District 3	2,883	227	11	100	5.3	92	13:1
	Orangeburg Consolidated School District 4	3,766	249	12	99.6	4.4	89	15:1
	Orangeburg Consolidated School District 5	6,629	363	21	99.5	5	95	18:1
Southern University and A & M College	East Baton Rouge Parish	42,609	3033	103	96	6.7	983	14:1
	West Baton Rouge Parish	3,884	355	11	82.3	2.3	59	11:1

Note: Data from the U.S. Department of Education Civil Rights Data Collection (CRDC), which collects and reports data on key education and civil rights issues in public school. (https://ocrdata.ed.gov/) (Survey year: 2015)

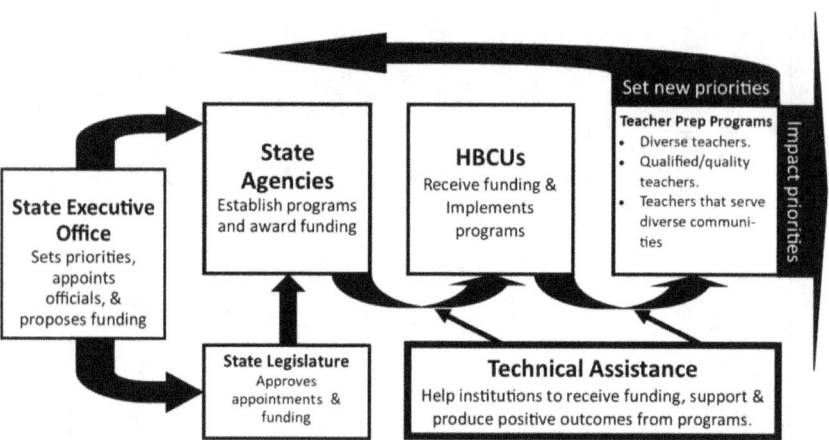

FIGURE 1.1   A model illustrating the relationship between state government and the ability of HBCUs to implement robust teacher preparation programs that can diversify the teacher workforce with qualified teachers that serve the unique needs of various school districts

Understanding formal HBCU structures from this perspective enabled our research team to explore new dynamics in the causes and implications for HBCUs producing more underrepresented education majors who eventually become teachers.

The study used secondary data analysis and interviews with school of education deans to help state executives, lawmakers, agencies, and nongovernmental organizations understand the best ways to support HBCUs with teacher preparation programs. The following model illustrates the relationship between various important entities and the ability of HBCUs to implement robust teacher preparation programs that can diversify that workforce with qualified teachers that serve the unique needs of disparate school districts. Investing in HBCU teacher preparation programs also helps to set new priorities for the institutions and school districts.

2.2   Method

Participants: For this investigation, we compared four HBCUs with teacher preparation programs: the University of Arkansas Pine Bluff; Claflin University; Alcorn State University; and Southern University Baton Rouge. We explored each institution's characteristics and interviewed education deans for this report.

Institutional characteristics were derived from our observations and analyses of data from the Integrated Postsecondary Education Data System (IPEDS). IPEDS consists of nine interrelated survey instruments that are gathered annually over three collection periods (fall, winter, and spring). Specific contributing factors that we explored with IPEDS prior to our interviews included enrollment patterns, retention and graduation rates, funding, human capital, and infrastructure. This information gave us context for the interviews that was not recorded in our report. Secondary data sources were also used to understand racial disparities in the school districts adjacent to the participating HBCUs.

We interviewed senior administrators at four HBCU schools and then used an external entity to transcribe the interview data. Upon receipt of the interview transcription, the research team embarked on understanding the qualitative data through a series of activities that included organizing the data, generating themes and patterns, searching for alternative explanations for the data, and writing the report. Researchers drew on this analysis to further identify preliminary themes and create coding categories.

Qualitative data analysis revealed five primary themes and three secondary themes. Themes address institutional strengths and needs, as well as the needs of the surrounding districts and communities, against the backdrop of state mandates and professional standards.

2.3   Theme 1: Partnerships

The interviewees emphasized the importance of establishing and maintaining relationships between institutions, districts and the community. One dean said, "You can't assume that a university can fully prepare teachers, there has got to be a partnership." Another shared a similar sentiment: "It is not the university going to save the district. The district can do a whole lot to help us improve our teacher education program and our other programs on campus too."

Education deans overall reported having strong relationships with the districts. "We look at the district as an extension of the university and the university as an extension of the district. In service teachers and faculty are colleagues who happen to work in different places," as one dean described their connection.

These strong relationships were in part attributed to the size of communities being small and near to each other. Many deans commented on the closeness of the community, stating that "everybody knows each other." The education deans also noted being close with the district superintendents. Further, many of the principles, school leaders, and teachers within the public school districts were trained at the respective HBCU within their community.

Education deans noted serving on an advisory board or co-op group with district superintendents, where the superintendents advise them on district needs. In addition, schools of education are engaging with the districts in "grow-your-own" initiatives. With this, districts reach within their own areas and provide scholarships and resources to recruit and train their own teachers so that they would then come back and teach in the districts.

Also, this initiative targets teachers on waivers and universities assist them in obtaining teacher certifications. Continued efforts are needed to strengthen relationships, including efforts to increase parent involvement and political engagement. One dean said, "The battle is bigger than the school and the university."

2.4 Theme 2: Continued Professional Development

The interviews revealed a consensus regarding the importance of professional development for continuous growth on the part of both the districts and HBCUs. A lack thereof is a downside; as one dean noted, "we don't invest enough in professional development and then we get mad that people keep doing things the way they have always done them." They continued, "you must go somewhere and learn something new."

Universities have made efforts to provide professional development for in-service teachers. These various opportunities have allowed, at the district level, development of growth plans and modules for working with English language learners, preparation for licensure exams, and have included offering certificate programs. As mentioned above, the need for professional development is twofold.

One dean said, "we need the input of experienced teachers early on in the process to make sure that what we are doing at the university makes sense and that it reflects what the teachers have to do in the school." Continual nurturing and support is necessary for novice teachers, those students who recently completed their studies and are entering their first years of teaching. This continued grooming process leads to preparing an effective teacher.

2.5 Theme 3: College Preparedness

Students are not entering college prepared to reach certain benchmarks such as passing standardized exams. Also, students' competitiveness as college applicants is thwarted. To address this, HBCUs have offered dual enrollment, ACT prep, and mentorship programs that will enable marginalized students to be prepared for college. Continued and targeted efforts are necessary, though, as noted in this statement:

> Generally a lot of schools don't know about these programs but if we are partnering with schools we will send it out and let them know that there is assistance in the state for students who are interested in enhancing their test scores on the ACT.

Another shared a similar experience:

> What I'm trying to encourage students to do is, it's just easier to do it while you're in high school, just try to make the grade on the ACT. We can work to try to get you where you need to score in order to get in teacher education.

Further, earlier-life interventions are necessary, as one dean noted: "Algebra 1 is now the gatekeeper." In significantly distressed districts, a pipeline exists; as one respondent said, "they don't go to middle school, they go to juvenile hall."

One dean argued that a substantial proportion of these students are there "because they are illiterate." There are several effective programs that address this issue, and respondents encouraged troubled districts to review what successful districts were doing and then institute those effective practices within their respective districts. "We just need to stop reinventing the wheel," one dean said.

2.6 *Theme 4: Standardized Exams*

Education deans shared challenges that arise with students passing examinations such as the ACT, Praxis, and licensure exams. States have mandated that students obtain certain examinations scores, which, in some cases, are significantly higher than average performance rates for African American students. As one dean expressed:

> The mean ACT score for Black students is 16 and you need a 22 to get into Teacher Education; we can never win. The public schools are not preparing our students to enter college or to have that 22 on the ACT, so we're always a step behind in preparation.

The students and the university are both at a disadvantage in that this issue significantly reduces eligible students for HBCU teacher education programs, and it in turn affects enrollment rates. "Passing Praxis Core has been the hurdle that shrinks the number of teachers that we produce every year," one dean noted. Effects are seen with student retention as well.

As one dean explained:

> We are finding that a number of students, once they get here, begin to hear horror stories about Praxis and things students tell them so some of them become so fearful that they decide to change their major at the outset. They won't even attempt to pursue a degree in Education because they fear the idea of taking the Praxis.

Students also face difficulty passing licensure exams. The exams are numerous and expensive, which presents challenges for students. One dean noted, "it costs as much to take one area as it does to take all of the areas at the same time."

The interviews revealed a shared concern that the content areas tested within these standardized examinations do not correlate with what candidates will do in the classroom and are not representative of real-life situations within the field. In addition, the exams neither adequately measure candidates' capabilities nor do they predict candidates' success and subsequent performance as a teacher. Education deans noted a lack of empirical evidence as to how mandated passing scores and content areas are determined. Also notable was that the mandated standards change often and seemingly after some success is made in raising exam performance rates. In the following statement, one dean shared their experience:

> I don't want to say it's intentional but it just seems to be very coincidental that we make progress and then all of the sudden the standards change. The passing score that you need increases and then you have again a large number of African American and students of color who don't pass and then students in rural areas that don't pass.

2.7 Theme 5: Broadening Understanding beyond Mandated Content Areas

The education deans highlighted their shared mission to produce teachers who are highly qualified to teach in high-risk rural or urban school districts. To accomplish this, it is imperative that teacher candidates possess an understanding beyond content knowledge to be truly effective. Moreover, in addition to the mandated content areas, the deans discussed the shared expectation that their teacher candidates excel in areas related to social justice and socio-emotional learning.

This, as one dean explained, means "taking into account more affective dimensions of the student, of understanding nonverbal cues from the learner's perspective. What that means is designing instruction that really does meet the individual needs of the learner." Teachers need to have a lot more socio-emotional effectiveness, resourcefulness, compassion, and a better understanding of the world and of diverse cultures.

A common strength of HBCUs is that "the faculty is extremely committed to helping teacher candidates understand that they are teaching a content area that is critical but at the same time have to pay attention to the family, the community, and again, generally, the other issues that kids bring in the school" said one dean. This ensures that teacher candidates understand what it truly takes to create the kind of environment in school where students are inspired to learn.

2.8   Secondary Themes

2.8.1   Institutional Strengths

The deans noted institutional strengths as well as program characteristics that enable successful teacher preparation. They reported receiving support from the alumni, community, and university administration. One said, "There is tremendous loyalty to the institution. We can always count on our alumni to support different school initiatives."

Another stated that their alumni are "one of the best in the country of all HBCUs in the nation." Regarding assistance from university administrations, one dean reported having "absolute support." The aid received at the university level was attributed to the university's realization that "education is the foundation of the university." One dean also noted that "[i]n terms of meeting the mandates of national and state accreditation, the university is very supportive of those."

Characteristic of HBCUs is the commitment of faculty and the quality of the training experiences offered. When highlighting their program, one dean said:

> We have over 600+ field experience hours before they student teach the last semester of their fourth year of college. Beginning field experience classes are in high-risk schools, so you can see the types of issues that teachers are dealing with, so your mind is really open when you get to your upper levels practicum and [with] student teaching, you're in the best practices.

Often the students in these programs view teaching as a way to give back to their communities. After students have completed the program, deans noted that they have had great success in assisting students obtain local job placements. One dean said:

> In most cases, if the school at which they are working has a vacancy the next year, they will already have a job at that school if that student wants to stay there. Beyond that, the rest of them, at the 100 percent level, have jobs in most cases before they even finish student teaching. We've done a good job of that.

2.8.2   Institutional Needs

Respondents emphasized institutional need for freedom, flexibility, and support. Teacher education program mandates currently do not allow for a lot of freedom, which has historically allowed for HBCUs to best meet their students' needs. One dean stated that their program must obtain "special permissions" to implement certain program objectives (e.g., student field experience placements in low-performing schools in surrounding communities) and felt that the program was "not trusted to understand which teachers are successful and which are having problems."

To address the restrictions placed on these programs, one dean suggested, "I think when people have programs that are innovative, cutting edge or creative, the policymakers need to allow them to pilot and maybe [allot] some funds to pilot."

Financial support is a continual need at HBCUs to address heightened mandates. As one dean said, "When you have professional schools that have to deal with accreditation issues, that deal with having to have highly qualified faculty, it's real important to have budgets that reflect that."

2.8.3 Needs of Teachers in Surrounding Districts

The surrounding districts faced challenges with recruiting and retaining quality teachers. The education deans attributed this to the low salaries and lack of incentives (like signing bonuses, housing assistance), which resulted in high attrition. In addition, teachers in STEM (science, technology, engineering, and math) areas presented a particularly high turnover rate. One dean said, "A lot of teachers in the STEM area may start off teaching in some of the rural districts but the goal is to get that experience and then move on to teaching a more affluent district. So, you have this constant high rate of attrition from the districts that need teachers the most."

2.9 *Summary*

Interviews with HBCU education deans highlighted the drivers of and barriers to teacher preparation at HBCUs. The first theme, Partnerships, discussed how strong relationships with the surrounding school districts served as an institutional strength that drove success. The second theme, Continued Professional Development, emphasized the need for continuous growth within teacher education on the part of both the districts and HBCUs. The third theme, College Preparedness, addressed the barrier that HBCU teacher education programs face, which is that students are not being prepared to enter the institutions that have historically served them and, more specifically, the HBCU teacher preparation programs. The fourth theme, Standardized Exams, addresses another barrier facing students, specifically the passing of examinations to satisfy program enrollment and/or completion requirements. The fifth theme, Broadening Understanding beyond Mandated Content Areas, highlighted a drive to train quality teachers by challenging their candidates to develop an understanding beyond the course content.

Several secondary themes brought more context and clarity to the primary issues facing HBCU schools of education. Institutional Strengths discussed various characteristics of the institutions and the programs that have served as positive factors in their efforts to advance their programs. Institutional Needs discussed the need for more freedom, flexibility, and financial support to adequately address the needs of the programs and the surrounding districts. Needs of the Surrounding Districts discussed the challenges that districts face with recruiting and retaining quality teachers.

The discussed themes allowed for a better understanding of the challenges facing and successes of HBCU teacher education programs in producing quality teachers. Moreover, they provided insight into the ways that HBCUs can exert more leadership in their surrounding districts to help resolve some of the educational issues that particularly plague African American students, who are underrepresented in general.

3 Strategic Priorities for HBCUs and Teacher Prep

3.1 *Recruiting and Retaining Teachers*

Hiring experienced and highly effective teachers from diverse backgrounds is essential to creating an equitable learning environment. According to Partee (2014), Black students face lower prospects of having an effective teacher versus white students. Majority Black schools typically have more inexperienced educators, reducing opportunities to achieve.

However, the deeper problem lies not in teachers' experience but in their diversity. Children of color will compose about half of all PK–12 students (Jackson & Kohli, 2016). Meanwhile, Black men represent less than 2% of the teaching force, with a student body that is 7% Black male. By comparison, white female teachers comprise 63% of the teaching force, with a student body that is 27% white female. Considering the entire student body, the United States has one white female teacher for every fifteen students and one Black male teacher for every 534 students (Toldson, 2019). There are several major implications of the underrepresentation of Black teachers in US schools.

The recruiting of teachers of color is complicated by several issues. First, there is a pay gap between white and Black teachers' earnings. Second, educators of color face negative biases from their colleagues. Third, majority-minority public schools typically have heightened responsibilities and lower resource allocation (Bland, Church, & Luo, 2014). Ingersoll and May (2016) consider the shortage of minority teachers "a major civil rights issue" (p. 1), and statistics indicate that over 40% of US schools do not employ a single Black teacher (Jackson & Kohli, 2016). To improve the situation, researchers recommend enhancing the hiring process, bolstering teachers' preparation, and improving educators' working conditions (Podolsky, Kini, Bishop, & Darling-Hammond, 2017).

Currently, the demand for teachers is higher than the supply. There are several explanations:
1. Rising PK–12 student enrollment (Berry & Shields, 2017).
2. Many schools are struggling to restore teaching positions that underwent severe cuts during the Great Recession.
3. The number of people entering the profession is constantly dropping. According to statistical data, there has been a 35% drop in teacher preparation program enrollment between 2009 and 2014 (Berry & Shields, 2017).
4. The US loses about 8% of its educators yearly, with the attrition level being nearly two times higher than in top-performing countries such as Singapore or Finland.

There are several steps that authorities should take to improve teacher retention. Studies have considered initiating paid teacher residency projects as a viable approach to promoting the supply of professionals (Barth, Dillon, Hull, & Higgins, 2016). Also, programs to forgive all or part of educators' student loans have the potential to attract more teachers. Creating effective peer teams of minority teachers is also a promising trend (Dee & Goldhaber, 2017). Therefore, it is possible to conclude that while recruiting teachers involves numerous difficulties, retention rates could considerably improve under certain circumstances.

3.2 *Teachers' Cultural Competence*

Students' growing diversity necessitates that teachers develop the competence to meet the needs of the different races and ethnicities in their classes (Alismail, 2016). As Goldenberg (2014) notes, the common phrase "closing the achievement gap" involves more than aptitude. It is important to "reframe" achievement "in terms of opportunity" (Goldenberg, 2014, p. 112). Low cultural competence among teachers worsens the disadvantages associated with segregated school environments.

Culturally sensitive teachers empathize with their students' experiences and are more likely to build a positive perception of learners' academic potential (Dilworth & Coleman, 2014). Researchers thus note that the underrepresentation of teachers of color reduces access to culturally competent educators for African American students. According to Dilworth and Coleman (2014), Black teachers have a higher degree of social consciousness and are more committed to educating African American students. Considering this evidence, one can see how HBCUs are central to creating more opportunities for students of color to become fully engaged in the learning process.

One approach to enhancing cultural diversity is eliminating institutional colorblindness (Hachfeld et al., 2015). When colorblind teachers claim to treat every student equally, they choose to treat them by the cultural values of white learners. Research demonstrates that white educators are prone to agreeing with colorblind beliefs. On the contrary, teachers of color more often choose multicultural approaches. Hachfeld et al. (2015) report that multicultural-oriented educators demonstrate more pedagogically effective problem-solving tactics and choose less harsh disciplinary measures for their students. Thus, a viable approach to achieving cultural diversity is to increase the number of Black teachers in schools. As Jackson and Kohli (2016) note, teachers of color are well-suited for African American students since they have a deep understanding of "the cultural experiences of these learners" (p. 1).

4 Conclusions

Educating teachers and shaping their professional worldviews starts in college, so HBCUs should shape their teacher preparation programs to address the needs that have been outlined herein. First, based on the literature, it is necessary to increase opportunities for Black students, especially males, to become teachers. However, many obstructive policies stand in the way of opening such opportunities. Sealey-Ruiz and Greene (2015) call these obstructions "educational genocide" (p. 55). State policies should be race-conscious, rather than race-neutral, to expand opportunities to Black education students at HBCUs. HBCUs likewise need the autonomy to advance a curriculum that is social justice–oriented and integrates multiculturalism into teacher preparation (Sleeter, 2016). Since many predominately white institutions use colorblind approaches to teaching, we need HBCUs to develop new systems that appreciate the growing diversity of this nation.

In the HBCU-adjacent school districts that we surveyed, African American students were the majority and faced the worst inequities. Therefore, it is crucial to increase opportunities for Black teachers to implement their knowledge and cultural experience in schools. Recommendations to improve the possibilities of future teachers of color should not uphold the status quo but should germinate from the principles of critical race theory (Milner & Laughter, 2014; Sleeter, 2016). Milner and Laughter (2014) suggest three policies that can alleviate racial disparities in schools. The first policy involves reforming teacher education programs to focus on a deeper study of race. The second recommends including a more profound analysis of poverty. Finally, the third policy advocates investigating the connection between race and poverty during teacher preparation programs.

Banks (2015) notes that it is crucial to add more cultural experiences to the curriculum so that future teachers could be multicultural. By doing this, higher educational establishments will promote equal opportunities for all school children under the guidance of unbiased teachers. Additionally, the education community should "take collective ownership" of the recruitment, preparation, and support of new teachers (Banks, 2015, p. 60).

Finally, colleges and universities should alter their teacher preparation programs so that they match the needs of young educators. As Dilworth and Coleman (2014) remark, there are currently many programs that do not offer a sufficient degree of mentorship, which is one of the core elements of teacher retention. There are thus many ways in which colleges and universities could change their teacher preparation programs to match both teachers' and students' needs. It is essential to introduce such changes to the education system in order to alleviate racial disparities in US schools.

Black students are dealing with racism and bias, implicitly and explicitly, from school personnel, including teachers and administrators. These racial biases manifest in (a lack of) enrichment opportunities like gifted programs and AP classes, racial disparities in discipline, and uneven expressions of acceptance, compassion, respect, and admiration from teachers and administrators. This book calls for diversifying the teacher workforce as well as using state resources, such as HBCUs, to strengthen diversity efforts.

State higher education executives should consider the causes and implications of teacher workforces in HBCU-adjacent school districts having significantly different racial and other demographic characteristics than the students they serve. In addition, more information about current teachers is needed to determine what resources are necessary to help them provide quality instruction to students.

Most district- and state-level recommendations to improve teacher quality focus on the academic capabilities of the teachers. However, the variance in teachers' ability to teach students may not be a function of academic ineptitude. Sufficient research evidence exists to suggest that social and emotional characteristics separate effective teachers from ineffective teachers. Teachers who are motivated, empathetic, genuine, and exhibit care and compassion can connect with students in a way that helps them to better engage in the learning process.

State higher education executives should construct a profile that captures all of the characteristics of an effective teacher that can teach a diverse student body, one that extends beyond academic preparation, and develop policies and procedures to encourage more teachers who fit the profile. The deans and directors of HBCU schools of education were clear that state requirements for admission to teacher education programs and certifications were out of step with the needs of diverse learners.

5 Recommendations

1. State higher education executives should explicitly recommend an audit of teacher certification requirements to determine if biases in teacher credentialing contribute to the lack of diversity in the teacher workforce and place an unfair burden on HBCU teacher preparation programs.
2. State higher education executives should underscore the role that HBCUs play in preparing principals and counselors to cultivate an environment for teachers to develop cultural competence and enhance empathy and respect for students.
3. State higher education executives should identify potential biases in any new strategies to elevate standards for licensure. Newly implemented teacher licensure revisions in the state of Florida recently resulted in hundreds of teachers of color being fired, including those with high ratings.
4. State higher education executives should recommend cultural competency training for teachers state-wide and endorse HBCUs with schools of education to provide continuing education training for in-service teachers. Culturally competent teachers invite open and honest dialogue about race and ethnicity in trainings, supervision and interprofessional dialogue, after confronting their own biases, assumptions, and prejudices about other racial or ethnic groups. Culturally competent teachers use professional resources and activities to develop specific skills to accommodate racially and ethnically diverse students.

References

Alismail, H. A. (2016). Multicultural education: Teachers' perceptions and preparation. *Journal of Education and Practice, 7*(11), 139–146.

Banks, T. (2015). Teacher education reform in urban educator preparation programs. *Journal of Education and Learning, 4*(1), 60–71.

Barth, P., Dillon, N., Hull, J., & Higgins, B. H. (2016). *Fixing the holes in the teacher pipeline: An overview of teacher shortages.* Center for Public Education. http://www.fsba.org/wp-content/uploads/2016/06/CPE-Overview-of-Teacher-Shortages-April-2016.pdf

Berry, B., & Shields, P. M. (2017). Solving the teacher shortage: Revisiting the lessons we've learned. *Phi Delta Kappan, 98*(8), 8–18.

Black, S. E., Cortes, K. E., & Lincove, J. A. (2015). *Apply yourself: Racial and ethnic differences in college application*. National Bureau of Economic Research. http://users.nber.org/~cortesk/NBER_w21368_apply.pdf

Bland, P., Church, E., & Luo, M. (2014). Strategies for attracting and retaining teachers. *Administrative Issues Journal: Education, Practice, and Research, 4*(1).

Bryant, R. T.-A-F. (2015). *College preparation for African American students: Gaps in the high school educational experience*. https://vtechworks.lib.vt.edu/bitstream/handle/10919/83649/CollegePreparationAfricanAmerican.pdf?sequence=1&isAllowed=y

Carter, P. L., Skiba, R., Arredondo, M. I., & Pollock, M. (2016). You can't fix what you don't look at: Acknowledging race in addressing racial discipline disparities. *Urban Education, 52*(2), 207–235.

Dee, T. S., & Goldhaber, D. (2017). *Understanding and addressing teacher shortages in the United States*. The Hamilton Project. https://www.hamiltonproject.org/assets/files/understanding_and_addressing_teacher_shortages_in_us_pp.pdf

Dilworth, M. E., & Coleman, M. J. (2014). *Time for a change: Diversity in teaching revisited*. https://vtechworks.lib.vt.edu/bitstream/handle/10919/84025/ChangeDiversityTeaching.pdf?sequence=1

Flashman, J. (2014). Friend effects and racial disparities in academic achievement. *Sociological Science, 1*, 260–276.

Gamoran, A. & An, B. P. (2016). Effects of school segregation and school resources in a changing policy context. *Educational Evaluation and Policy Analysis, 38*(1), 43–64.

Goldenberg, B. M. (2014). White teachers in urban classrooms: Embracing non-white students' cultural capital for better teaching and learning. *Urban Education, 49*, 111–144. http://dx.doi.org/10.1177/0042085912472510

Grissom, J. A., & Redding, C. (2016). Discretion and disproportionality: Explaining the underrepresentation of high-achieving students of color in gifted programs. *AERA Open, 2*(1), 1–25.

Groeger, L., Waldman, A., & Eads, D. (2018). *Miseducation: Is there racial inequality at your school?* https://projects.propublica.org/miseducation/

Hachfeld, A., Hahn, A., Schroeder, S., Anders, Y., & Kunter, M. (2015). Should teachers be colorblind? How multicultural and egalitarian beliefs differentially relate to aspects of teachers' professional competence for teaching in diverse classrooms. *Teaching and Teacher Education, 48*, 44–55.

Haddix, M. M. (2017). Diversifying teaching and teacher education: Beyond rhetoric and toward real change. *Journal of Literacy Research, 49*(1), 141–149.

Ingersoll, R., & May, H. (2016). *Minority teacher recruitment, employment, and retention: 1987 to 2013*. https://www2.calstate.edu/impact-of-the-csu/teacher-education/Documents/minority_teacher_recruitment_employment_retention_brief.pdf

Jackson, T. O., & Kohli, R. (2016). Guest editors' introduction: The state of teachers of color. *Equity & Excellence in Education, 49*(1), 1–8.

Meyer, J., & Rowan, B. (1977). Institutionalized organizations: Formal structure as myth and ceremony. *American Journal of Sociology, 83*(2), 340–363.

Milner, H. R., & Laughter, J. C. (2014). But good intentions are not enough: Preparing teachers to center race and poverty. *The Urban Review, 47*(2), 341–363.

Morris, E. W., & Perry, B. L. (2016). The punishment gap: School suspension and racial disparities in achievement. *Social Problems, 63*(1), 68–86.

Munk, T. E., McMillan, M. M., & Lewis, N. R. (2014). Compositional effects, segregation and test scores: Evidence from the national assessment of educational progress. *Review of Black Political Economy, 41*(4), 433–454.

Partee, G. L. (2014). *Attaining equitable distribution of effective teachers in public schools.* https://files.eric.ed.gov/fulltext/ED561064.pdf

Podolsky, A., Kini, T., Bishop, J., & Darling-Hammond, L. (2017). Sticky schools: How to find and keep teachers in the classroom. *Phi Delta Kappan, 98*(8), 19–25.

Reardon, S. F. (2016). School segregation and racial academic achievement gaps. *RSF: The Russell Sage Foundation Journal of the Social Sciences, 2*(5), 34–57.

Sealey-Ruiz, Y., & Greene, P. (2015). Popular visual images and the (mis)reading of Black male youth: A case for racial literacy in urban pre-service teacher education. *Teaching Education, 26*(1), 55–76.

Skiba, R. J., Arredondo, M. I., & Rausch, M. K. (2014). *New and developing research on disparities in discipline.* http://www.njjn.org/uploads/digital-library/OSF_Discipline-Disparities_Disparity_NewResearch_3.18.14.pdf

Sleeter, C. E. (2016). Critical race theory and the whiteness of teacher education. *Urban Education, 52*(2), 155–169.

Tolbert, P., & Zucker, L. (1996). The institutionalization of institutional theory. In S. Clegg, C. Hardy, & W. Nord (Eds.), *Handbook of organization studies* (pp. 175–190). Sage.

Toldson, I. A. (2019). *No BS (bad stats): Black people need people who believe in Black people enough not to believe every bad thing they hear about Black people.* Brill Sense.

CHAPTER 2

Building Meaningful HBCU and PK–20 Partnerships beyond the Ivory Tower

Allyson L. Watson

This chapter provides a comprehensive overview of building meaningful PK–20 partnerships within and external to the university setting, sharing best practices and helpful insights regarding developing partnerships so that the reader can identify transferrable points across institutions. The chapter cites specific examples from one HBCU that can apply to peer institutions both public and private. I analyze various factors pertaining to increasing enrollment and employability, along with highlighting federally funded programs to build other external partnerships.

Since institutional partnerships strengthen strategies for building better teaching professionals, which in turn helps produce nationally competitive PK–20 graduates, specific ideas are noted around developing such seamless relationships with HBCU African American graduates in PK–12 and postsecondary education. The chapter also highlights how various organizations could benefit from HBCU partnerships since they would get qualified personnel, which increases workforce diversification.

1   Introduction

It is critical for universities to build community outside the walls of the ivory tower. Teacher preparation programs have to develop partnerships external to the institution for viability and to increase capacity among the graduates. Institutional partnerships enrich the building of better teaching professionals. Many HBCUs began as normal schools, aiming to educate and improve the Black community by providing educational resources to prepare them for jobs as teachers. Alabama A&M, the University of Arkansas at Pine Bluff, Bowie State University, Howard University, Hampton University, Florida A&M University, and many others started with the mission of educating freed African Americans to prepare them for gainful employment. HBCUs started close to the signing of the Emancipation Proclamation in 1863, and the majority were founded between 1865 and the early 1900s. Leaders at these institutions developed partnerships with political figures, Quakers, abolitionists, and champions for what we would historically and presently consider equal rights and equity for African American citizens (Roselle, Hands, & Cahill, 2020). These key partnerships helped promote educational entities hundreds of years ago that are still standing and thriving as nationally prominent universities that are loved and cherished by alumni across the country.

Given that HBCUs fulfill a greater call and purpose when it comes to developing graduates who can compete nationally for careers, current trends in educational partnerships indicate an increased urgency for higher education institutions. Educational leaders at HBCUs are pressed to seek partnerships and secure external funding (Radina et al., 2018), as this will create more opportunities for graduates and often break cycles of poverty by providing a new trajectory for first-generation college students. HBCU leaders must reimagine how their programs can thrive with expanded partnerships, focusing on those in traditional settings and expanding to business, nonprofit organizations, and community groups.

2 Federal and Private Programs that Benefit from Partnerships with HBCUs

Federal Title III funding is grant-based support for institutions of higher education with at least 50% of their students served showing unmet needs. The institution must be accredited or seeking accreditation, and the guidelines for students who demonstrate unmet needs are articulated in Title IV of the *Higher Education Act*, which identifies the number of students enrolled receiving Pell Grants. This funding aims to improve academic quality, institutional management, and fiscal stability. While it is not a PK–20 partnership, Title III does provide substantial financial support for eligible institutions committed to improving students' academic success, and HBCUs may thus use this funding to strengthen their resources and academic programs to get their students career and workforce ready (Radina et al., 2018). Such partnerships could collaborate with state and local agencies, aligning academic enrichment with student service programs to create a streamlined college-to-career pathway.

One example of how this could be achieved in an HBCU is through educator career preparation programs. Suppose an HBCU leader develops a teaching preparation enrichment program with an articulated intervention plan and quarterly measures of academic success. In this case, they may use the funding platform to share with state and local educational entities how these measures created optimal results for pre-service teachers and teaching candidates. By sharing how the intervention and academic program strengthened candidates, those external stakeholders will be more likely to promote the academic program and graduates from the program for PK–12 positions. State departments of education aim to increase graduates from within the state and track longitudinal data for candidates graduating from educator preparation programs who work in state PK–12 schools.

An added benefit of partnerships for HBCUs is the potential to increase scholarly grant funding through additional federal bodies such as the National Science Foundation, the National Aeronautics and Space Administration, and the US Department of Justice. Federally funded grant programs look for in-depth funding proposals that align with national research agendas. In the COVID-19 climate, there are disparaged African American communities that could benefit greatly from the assistance of federally funded programs that are written and authored by HBCU scholars. These partnerships can change the trajectories of many marginalized people and add positive narratives to the academic literature that come from scholars who hold the communities and people with high regard. The fund sourced through various HBCU partnerships can be used for either purchasing or leasing the scientific laboratories to allow students from poor communities to pursue STEM (science, technology, engineering, and math) courses.

In most cases, these courses are not available at HBCUs due to a lack of proper equipment to fully train students and equip them with relevant job skills. Adequate funds can be used to improve or maintain laboratories and instruction facilities (Bracey, 2017) as well as support faculty exchange and develop academic instruction in programs where Black students are underrepresented. Additionally, proper funding will allow for effective administration, mutual sharing of facilities, improve and establish new offices, and enhance programs focusing on teachers' education so that more Black teachers who graduate can work in the PK–12 schools. These measures will enable more students of color to join colleges and universities.

The 21st Century Community Learning Centers were developed after the *No Child Left Behind Act* of 2001 was signed into law, linking PK–12 schools with universities, businesses, and nonprofits to mitigate barriers for children in poverty. This partnership model has been implemented across the country, particularly in school districts with large numbers of Title I schools, to improve academic achievement, enrichment services, and family literacy and educational development. One of the community partnership stipulations is that there must be a higher education entity represented, and so while this partnership model's primary benefactor is the public school student, the colleges, schools, and businesses involved receive the reciprocal benefit of extending resources. Within the realm of 21st Century Community Centers and schools, HBCU teacher preparation programs can be significant partners and maintain meaningful relationships while building and promoting the teaching profession (Bracey, 2017).

For instance, at a school in Florida, for which the local HBCU and predominantly white institution (PWI) served as partner institutions, the elementary leader noticed the students categorized as English Language Learners (ELL) needed extra assistance during normal classroom instruction. The HBCU elementary education program held a state endorsement for elementary education majors, specifically ELL, and so the principal and university leaders partnered to develop a pre-service curriculum to conduct field experiences linked to their college ELL course. This partnership created synergy and success for the school, the student population, and the pre-service teachers. Within this arrangement, the pre-service teachers received guided, hands-on instruction, and the elementary students developed confidence and abilities by having enriched individual instruction.

3   Benefits of PK–12 and HBCU Partnership

There are numerous lessons that PK–12 schools can take from HBCUs regarding providing quality educational experiences for the students. It is possible to translate HBCUs' success into PK–12 schools by adopting and implementing HBCU best practices. For instance, nurturing support systems in PK–12 schools would promote interaction between the students and faculty. This can be attained by employing a diverse faculty and implementing strategies such as intrusive advising to develop a caring partnership with the PK–12 students. HBCU educators can also help PK–12 schools in incorporating and embracing African American culture and identity in curricula, assisting students in developing a strong sense of identity to facilitate their success.

Integrating HBCU best practices calls for district schools to invest in quality advising and support systems, which prevents students from falling through the cracks. PK–12 school districts and managing charters, particularly ones with significant proportions of minority groups, need to make deliberate efforts to hire more teachers of color who reflect the student body. PK–12 schools therefore need to take deliberate actions to instill culturally relevant pedagogy into daily instructional practices. Just like HBCUs, PK–12 schools need to provide learners with the autonomy to create affinity groups that anchor race and culture. Such measures will enable the schools to refute any beliefs about racial superiority and allow all PK–20 students to excel.

Incorporating HBCU teachings and culture into PK–12 schools helps cultivate pride among African American students and offers students of color hands-on mentorship beginning in kindergarten. Black students in PK–12 have long been marginalized, making them internalize negative stereotypes; HBCUs can be a game changer in PK–12 schools by pushing them to prioritize equity. Often, there is a big belief gap among Black students because of the difference in what they perceive they can achieve and their actual academic results in schools. The gains already made in early mentorship and pride-building initiatives demonstrate how HBCUs' transformative strategies can impart wisdom within the PK–12 education system.

4 How PK–20 Partnerships Can Increase Enrollment at HBCUs

States often have streamlined transfer programs between junior, community, and two-year colleges to state university institutions. For an HBCU that fits in the state university category, that partnership can help develop an efficient transfer process within programs that have existing articulation agreements. For private HBCUs, there are often challenges in developing articulation agreements or memoranda of understanding with junior, community, and two-year colleges, but these partnerships can lead to great rewards for both student and partnering institutions. To develop viable partnerships, HBCU leaders must position themselves as value-added contributors to external partners.

In many states, junior and two-year colleges seek to recruit and graduate students of color within their programs. Public- and private-sector HBCU leaders can demonstrate their commitment to increasing the presence of such students within workforce and professional settings by articulating data trends for graduating higher numbers of African American students in careers that have a critical shortage. Looking at historical data, many of the top ten HBCUs produce the highest number of African American teachers. PK–12 education presently shows a critical need for teachers and principals, with an even greater need in Title I and rural schools, where the student population is comprised largely of students of color. We understand that the likelihood of students of color in PK–12 schools earning a college degree is often predicated upon the number of teachers of color they have in the PK–12 experience.

Partnerships between PK–12 and HBCUs can also increase student enrollment in HBCU institutions. PK–12s should be committed to offering quality education to students at the middle and high school levels to ensure that they can achieve the required grades to enroll in HBCUs, and partnerships that facilitate interactions between secondary school teachers and university faculty could allow PK–12 educators to learn what is required in college and university education. Science and mathematics educators could attend workshops at HBCUs during the summers so that they can keep up to date on contemporary issues in STEM and consequently equip their learners with the skills to help them in their college and university education. In essence, such partnerships would increase students' enrollment to and completion rate once they join higher learning institutions, hopefully moving beyond a single directional flow of information from experts to students and instead becoming mutually beneficial (Miller, Haynes, & Pennington, 2015).

Similarly, a graduate student–university–school collaborative initiative could increase the number of students who enroll in HBCUs. Such a partnership entails placing graduate students from various HBCUs in STEM subjects in a one-year fellowship with practicing PK–12 mathematics and science educators. Graduates are supported to offer technical support and assistance to the middle and the high school teachers during their fellowship period. As a result, universities and colleges would actively help to develop PK–12 school curricula (Miller, Haynes, & Pennington, 2015). This would improve the delivery of science and mathematics at the high school level, and these essential skills would later be useful in HBCU institutions. With a smoother transition and armed with prerequisite knowledge in high schools, many students would feel more confident joining colleges and universities to pursue courses and occupations with a deficit number of professionals, such as the education sector.

5   How HBCU PK–12 Partnerships Can Enhance PK–12 Practice

Highly diverse schools and districts often turn to expert educators for pedagogical tools that are effective in urban school environments. Growth mindset strategy, response to intervention (RIT), the ethos of care, grit, and resilience have been studied by leading educational researchers on and for PK–12 students of color – but rarely by scholars of color. However, a significant amount of research on teacher efficacy, culturally responsive teaching, and teaching students of color with gifted exceptionalities (Ford, 2014; Gay, 2018; Ladson-Billings, 2020) has been written by scholars of color and is highly cited. How does this research translate to practice? How does it look in a classroom with a majority of African American students?

The suggestion is not that white scholars cannot provide meaningful and transferrable pedagogical practices based on the research. Instead, the reality is that these pedagogical practices may be best explained and demonstrated through leaders and educators at HBCUs who are products of or have taught in these school environments. HBCUs can provide professional development, guided instruction, and one-on-one coaching to new and early career teachers charged by the school district to carry out these practices within the classroom (Miller, Haynes, & Pennington, 2015). HBCUs and PWIs within the same city, town, or region may develop a partnership to establish research and practical guides to increase student achievement generally and especially to decrease the gap for African American students and Title 1 schools.

In a recent meeting within a mid-sized urban school district, a school board member invited members from the local HBCU and PWI to speak with Title 1 principals, clergy, and civic leaders. The PWI member spoke eloquently about the university's plan to increase scholarly activities, promote grant research, and use grant funding to purchase needed educational supplies and other items to benefit Title 1 schools. Additionally, the PWI possessed the resources to provide staffing and faculty service hours to instruct schoolteachers on how to use the materials (Ledoux & McHenry, 2008). The reciprocal agreement would allow the PWI to take the data and other information learned from the intervention and publish national research in journals, book chapters, and peer-reviewed presentations. Of course, the benefit to the Title 1 school was the ability to have materials that did not come out of their designated Title 1 budget. While this is extremely beneficial and will promote research related to students of color, there was a missing piece that the HBCU leader brought to the table.

The HBCU leader connected with the community shared the community's plight and the need to develop equity within Title 1 schools. This leader could speak to the spiritual, financial, and academic needs facing the community, but they also presented tangible ways to assist teachers and school leaders, sharing a vision that provided a collaborative way to improve the community. The HBCU leader offered the Title 1 principals and civic leaders the opportunity to work with faculty and pre-service teachers (Miller, Haynes, & Pennington, 2015) and extended in-kind resources, such as facilities, meeting spaces, and a STR2EAM (Science, Technology, Reading, Research, Engineering, and Mathematics) Innovation Lab for mini-lessons. Lastly, the HBCU leader committed to developing a "grow-your-own" program to create a PK–20 pipeline for the students in Title 1 schools who aspired to become teachers, counselors, and health and leisure fitness professionals. This program would allow a member of the HBCU to visit each Title 1 school and discuss educational opportunities and the importance of being a teacher.

While the PWI and HBCU offered different opportunities, they both contributed to African American PK–12 students' success. Moreover, the HBCU was in a unique position to increase college awareness, culturally responsive academic programs, and faculty, as well as offer scholars of color who would focus on students' success (Ledoux & McHenry, 2008). HBCU leaders need to recognize and promote their uniqueness and, furthermore, to use such partnerships to underscore the impact of the PK–12 classroom through college.

Many HBCUs have long positioned themselves as a viable option for alleviating disparities experienced in PK–12 schools. Even though they constitute only about 4% of the nation's colleges and universities, given the sparsity of Black teachers in PK–12 school systems – which significantly affects the number of students of color enrolling for college diplomas and degrees – the impact of HBCU support for PK–12 schools is indisputable. African Americans teachers who are HBCU graduates form a significant professional body to prepare PK–12 students for enrolling in HBCUs. In most of urban and rural districts, HBCUs can furnish schools with considerably higher percentages of teachers. HBCUs also offer other educational administration programs, which are essential to preparing a significant number of PK–12 principals who can instill strong self-belief and higher expectations for all.

Relatively few African American males enroll in colleges and universities, and this has been linked to low numbers of Black male teachers (Radina et al., 2018). Through partnering with PK–12 schools, HBCUs can supply many Black male educators to these institutions. But such a model needs proper funding by the federal government so that HBCUs can train more teachers.

In most cases, when Black teachers enter PK–12 schools, they must understand their roles within the new organizational culture. They therefore assume, as a classroom teacher, that assimilating within the existing groups is a problem. This problem can, however, be addressed if the PK–12 school systems partner with HBCUs as they are training professionally (Miller, Haynes, & Pennington, 2015). Doing so helps teachers acquire cultural knowledge of diverse groups and find it easier to work in such settings when fully employed. Also, this prior cultural knowledge and experience will enable Black teachers to instill HBCU values, foster inclusivity, and set higher expectations for both white and Black students.

HBCUs and the PK–20 partnership can also contribute to the success of Black PK–12 students by offering educators alternative routes to certification. Such programs should allow participants to start teaching while completing their educational requirements (Price & Been, 2018). Notably, this would likely attract a large pool of African American educators, who would enroll in P-12 schools to fill the existing gap. Any candidate who held a bachelor's degree and sought entry into the education profession could enroll in the program without necessarily completing the four-year traditional preparation. These educators could serve high-need subject fields such as sciences and mathematics, as well as in schools that have staffing gaps.

Collaboration between HBCU and PK–20 institutions would increase staffing levels in PK–12 schools with majority African American students. About 18% of public school educators enter PK–12 schools through alternative programs and certifications (Price & Been, 2018), and further examination by race indicates that many African American follow this route. It is essential to recognize HBCUs' contribution to PK–12 programming by providing teachers with the flexibility to study while teaching in underserved communities.

While it is uncontested that alternative certification has increased the diversity of qualified teachers in PK–12 schools, program results can vary in terms of teacher retention and preparedness because each state determines its requirements for approved alternative certification (Fakayode et al., 2017). Due to such mixed results, there is a need to involve both HBCUs and PK–12 institutions in policymaking to standardize program qualifications.

Collaboration between HBCUs and PK–12s should likewise strive to mentor and prepare Black students for service in teaching. For example, Clemson University built a widely adopted MISTER (Mentors Instructing Students Towards Effective Role Models) program that focused on Black male graduates to improve Black teachers' enrollment in poorly performing PK-12 schools (Smith et al., 2017).

6 How Can HBCUs Establish PK–20 Partnerships That Lead to Employment Opportunities for Graduates?

Public and private school systems' ultimate rationale is to prepare students with developmentally appropriate measures that lead to college, career, and/or trade preparedness. HBCUs and the educational preparation programs aim for the same goals at the postsecondary level. Fruitful partnerships to merge PK–12 into PK–20 meet the elementary and secondary sector goals and provide preparation for postsecondary matriculation through graduation.

Partnerships between HBCUs and PK–20 can also increase employment opportunities for graduates from colleges and universities via student internships. While most of colleges and universities offer the theoretical part of studies to students, partnerships between HBCUs and local organizations can provide the graduates with avenues to apply their skills and gain practical experience for future employment opportunities (Miller, Haynes, & Pennington, 2015). Notably, collaboration between HBCUs and community organizations makes it easier for students to apply for internships, which increases graduates' employability (Miller, Haynes, & Pennington, 2015). Partnerships between

PK–20s and HBCUs can thus nurture professionals ready for job market opportunities, including addressing workforce deficiencies in particular professions.

HBCU collaboration with organizations could furthermore improve undergraduates' employability. HBCUs could form associations with companies that recognize HBCU graduates for employment opportunities. Establishing good relationships between universities and large organizations can help HBCUs to develop tailored curricula that meet organizations' needs – for example, technology companies could help the institution to offer relevant courses. Universities and colleges could then choose to alter their programs to supply graduates that could easily be absorbed into job markets.

HBCUs can also prepare final-year students to become valuable employees and to meet employers' demands. However, this task would not be possible without organizational partnerships, as colleges need to understand the essential skills and expertise required for graduates' employability. Through such partnerships, students can become familiar with principles and concepts that might not be part of the regular university or college education. For instance, collaboration with a local tech firm would familiarize students with computing languages and principles not taught in college.

Many students lack sufficient information on internship opportunities. However, HBCUs can develop memoranda of understanding with PK–20 partners to recognize existing job market gaps and to train students with the required skills. This approach enables tremendous growth in the curriculum while informing students of current opportunities.

For instance, Consortium Enabling Cybersecurity Opportunities & Research (CECOR) partners with several universities and plays a crucial role in providing exposure to computer science careers, demonstrating what it takes to be a cyber-security researcher, and so forth (Miller, Haynes, & Pennington, 2015). In this process, students can ground their academics in their career goals. There are hundreds of thousands of students, ranging from kindergarten to college undergraduates, who have been impacted by PK–20–industry partnerships over the years. Single universities may have difficulties accessing such opportunities, but with a close working strategy, many, including HBCUs, can have their graduating students benefit from the program.

Education and training programs and especially PK–12 summer internship programs help merge PK–20 education with training boot camps, through which young students can be taught essential professional skills. Such partnerships have led to the creation of more than ten new cybersecurity labs within HBCUs and introduced more than three thousand students to STEM programs. Without such a working relationship, most HBCU graduating students would have struggled or stayed unemployed a little longer. Because of such partnerships, more and more people will join the STEM workforce.

By establishing working partnerships with companies and PK–20 partners, HBCUs can help students gain through internships and job placements once they graduate. In return, corporate partners can create skills-specific centers within HBCU institutions. For example, coding and designing are critical skills in the market. Partnering with established companies and PK–20 institutions helps to develop workforce opportunities for learners of different ages. Such collaboration helps create a pipeline of professionals while also addressing racial equity and justice initiatives to tackle systemic job market barriers for the people of color, hence advancing economic equality. Existing partnerships have already introduced thousands of HCBU students to app coding and enhanced students' creativity, which is essential in the job market.

7 Recommendations and Best Practices for HBCUs Seeking Meaningful PK–20 Partnerships

To truly underscore the commitment to building meaningful partnerships beyond the ivory tower, HBCU leaders have to invest resources to develop and promote these partnerships. Every teacher education program in schools and colleges across the nation has a designee who places interns, organizes field experiences, and communicates with PK–12 stakeholders. That role is critical in building stronger and more fruitful partnerships. One best practice is to identify or hire a champion within the program who can tell the story of the HBCU. This individual can articulate institutional points of pride, share the program's strengths with external partners, and commit to excellence for all involved (Rubalcava, 2020).

Each HBCU can promote their image through their president, who must work closely with alumni associations and foundations. As a leader, the president is best positioned to effectively champion and articulate the HBCU with its partners, and since they control the organization, creating promotional strategies is paramount. The president must therefore address the goals and tasks of each leader and their responsibilities. Synchronizing these roles would create important synergies that enable the seamless flow of internal operations. Once inter-organization cooperation is developed, the president needs to seek external partners for program sustainability (Miller, Haynes, & Pennington, 2015). Such partnerships could be in knowledge-exchange areas or resource sharing, so that costs are kept down. Additionally, HBCU presidents need to address enrollment by presenting HBCU goals and objectives to PK–12 schools, promoting the college's image, and convincing them that the HBCU is the right institution in which to pursue their careers (Nkhata, 2018). The president should also work to improve relationships with funders for financial sustainability. Through developing strong collaborative strategies with internal and external stakeholders, HBCU continuity is guaranteed.

Second, the HBCU must ensure that their story and the institution's value-added progression is evident. A champion can often set the stage for burgeoning partnerships, but if the HBCU's website and social media is stagnant and outdated, it does not represent the best the HBCU has to offer. Dedicate time and talent to sharing meaningful contributions, alumni highlights, and points of pride frequently through social media and web-based content. Update old information and highlight new and exciting developments within the college. Create a vision around the institution's mission and values and demonstrate that to external partners.

HBCUs should promote their contribution to the achievement of educational equality in the country. They should present critical information and statistics indicating how the institution has worked to advance the US education system. A simple statement showing that HBCUs constitute 3% of American colleges and universities shows that they significantly impact the population. The website should also indicate that HBCUs produce more than 20% of all African American graduates and 25% of all Black Americans who graduate in STEM fields (Smith et al., 2017). This is crucial information since it shows that HBCUs are critical for future industries.

It is also important to note how HBCUs contribute to meeting the needs of first-generation and low-income students. On average, 80% of those who attend HBCUs are African Americans who need a college education to close the income gap. More than 70% of these students qualify for federal loans and grants to fund their education (Price & Been, 2018). Therefore, these institutions play a significant role in ensuring that vulnerable and needy students can acquire college and university education. Yet many do not publish this information on their websites. Promoting such important data would increase HBCU and PK–20 partnerships as well as students' enrollment in HBCUs.

A third and equally important best practice is to share HBCU faculty and student research with external stakeholders (Zenkov, Dennis, & Parker, 2019). This may include highlighting new grants, research reports, or PK–20 partnership practices with local news reporters to increase program visibility within the region and state. Colleges and universities play a crucial role in conducting research that impacts the entire community. HBCUs should thus facilitate collaboration between faculty and external organizations through community-based research, with studies aimed to benefit the participants either directly or indirectly. Such a contribution by HBCUs also increases their popularity and visibility among local communities.

Since most community-based research entails focus groups, surveys, and interactions with communities, the practice offers the institutions a unique opportunity to establish local partnerships. Most studies aim at solving problems in communities. Through such collaboration, university faculty can increase their connections with PK–20 schools (Price & Been, 2018). Another method of improving publicity for HBCUs entails sharing research findings with local news reporters, who are always interested in sharing intriguing results with the community and the state. When critical research findings come from a local HBCU, the community and students will want to be associated with the institution. This practice would thus increase HBCU visibility and publicity among local communities.

Fourth, HBCUs must aim to build trust with stakeholders and external partners. So often, in universities across the nation, PWI and others provide partnerships in name only. The notion of association equaling representation does not hold with PK–12 partners, who genuinely want to build a meaningful and reciprocal relationship. HBCUs should, therefore, develop a collaborative partnership with other minority institutions and especially with PWIs. Establishing joint partnerships with the minority-serving institutions and PWI is an effective and promising approach to strengthen stakeholders' trust and hence enhance the educational pipeline for learners, especially those who are currently underrepresented. However, such relationships should be established based on HBCUs' strength and success in producing a higher proportion of Black students who complete their studies in STEM categories (Nkhata, 2018). Therefore, forward-thinking HBCUs leaders should recognize the merits of nurturing stakeholder trust and local support – through, for example, community-based research projects that study health disparities and race and develop impactful solutions. Initiatives that recognize each institution's role and benefits are essential because to providing Black students with more access to academic opportunities, job openings, and professional training. Doing so also helps stakeholders appreciate HBCUs' transformational role and build strong community trust.

Finally, HBCUs have a wealth of alumni networks and resource-rich human capital. Furthermore, HBCU graduates span the education industry, from early career to tenured career professionals in leading positions. These are prime connections through which to build meaningful and rich PK–20 partnerships. HBCUs can promote academic excellence within PK–12 school districts by adopting a school program or classroom or participating in HBCU recruitment events. Impactful experiences like these keep HBCU programming at the forefront and increase the engagement to build and improve schools. Notably, HCBU are professional organizations, and their desires and need to maintain legitimacy are embedded in their organizational aims. HBCUs can foster collaboration between their alumni associations, presidents' offices, and foundations (Zenkov, Dennis, & Parker, 2019). Each of these units can enhance college status and legitimacy by acting as ambassadors in the corporate world, championing the college's mission, promoting its ethos and values to PK–12 graduates so that they can enroll in HBCU institutions. The rich networks of alumni can likewise help HBCUs to link their graduates to potential employers – more of the graduating class is immediately absorbed in the job market. Additionally, these professional organizations could collaborate with the college to inform them of skills required in the job market (Nkhata, 2018). With such information, the teaching staff can offer students the necessary knowledge and develop the right skills, creating a competitive advantage for HBCU graduates, who will be sought by employers. These alumni become problem solvers and great influencers on the enrollment into and continuity of HBCU operations.

8 Summary

HBCUs are responsible for producing thousands of African American baccalaureate graduates and the greatest number of African Americans with professional and doctoral degrees in the nation. HBCUs were founded amid the most tumultuous times in US history; they have overcome tremendous financial barriers and unequal measures of institutional merit, and they continue to be resilient and powerful in contributing to postsecondary success. It is advantageous for external stakeholders to partner with HBCUs. It is likewise beneficial for PK–12 school districts and nonprofit organizations to establish partnerships with HCBUs that offer reciprocal agreements for PK–12 initiatives and PK–20 career and workforce readiness. HBCUs have continually proven their dedication to students' personal and professional development within their programming. PK–20 partnerships with HBCUs can further this commitment. For HBCU leaders and educational stakeholders, it is hoped that this chapter ignites a sense of urgency to take the initiative and build stronger PK–20 and external partnerships, establishing meaningful alliances to create better opportunities for PK–12 and HBCU students.

References

Bracey, E. N. (2017). The significance of historically Black colleges and universities (HBCUs) in the 21st century: Will such institutions of higher learning survive? *American Journal of Economics and Sociology, 76*(3), 670–696.

Fakayode, S. O., Snipes, V., Kanipes, M. I., Mohammed, A. K., & Wilson, Z. S. (2017). Use of innovative pedagogies and creative partnership strategies to promote undergraduate STEM education at an HBCU. In Information and Research Management Association (Ed.), *Educational leadership and administration: Concepts, methodologies, tools, and applications* (pp. 1120–1151). IGI Global.

Ford, D. T. (2014). Segregation and the underrepresentation of Blacks and Hispanics in gifted education: Social inequality and deficit paradigms. *Roeper Review, 36*(3), 143–154.

Gay, G. (2018). *Culturally responsive teaching: Theory, research, and practice* (3rd ed.). Multicultural Education Series. Teachers College Press.

Ledoux, M. W., & McHenry, N. (2008). Pitfalls of school-university partnerships. *The Clearing House: A Journal of Educational Strategies, Issues and Ideas, 81*(4), 155–160.

Miller, J., Haynes, J., & Pennington, J. (2015). A partnership aimed at improving health and physical education at a rural school: Impacts on pupils, university students, teachers and academics. *Australian and International Journal of Rural Education, 25*(2), 56.

Nkhata, D. (2018). *Experiences of Black women students in science, technology, engineering, and mathematics at a historically white institution in the United States of America: A multiple case study* [Doctoral dissertation]. University of Oklahoma.

Price, T., & Been, N. (2018). HBCU collegiate students' reflections of a youth-adult partnership. *Journal of Park & Recreation Administration, 36*(1).

Radina, R., Aronson, B., Schwartz, T., Albright-Willis, J., Norval, B., Ross, G., & Wallace, M. (2018). A space for us too: Using youth participatory action research to center youth voices in school-university-community partnerships. *School-University Partnerships, 11*(4), 122–139.

Roselle, R., Hands, R. E., & Cahill, J. (2020). Daring greatly: School-university partnerships and the development of teacher leadership. *School-University Partnerships, 12*(4), 111–121.

Rubalcava, R. (2020). *UC San Diego Faculty partnerships with HBCUs help underrepresented students access graduate school*. UC San Diego News Service. https://ucsdnews.ucsd.edu/pressrelease/uc-san-diego-faculty-partnerships-with-hbcus-help-underrepresented-students-access-graduate-school

Smith, B. D., Marshall Jr, I., Anderson, B. E., & Daniels, K. K. (2017). A partnership forged: BSW students and service learning at a historically Black college and university (HBCU) serving urban communities. *Journal of Human Behavior in the Social Environment, 27*(5), 438–449.

Zenkov, K., Dennis, D. V., & Parker, A. K. (2019). Bless your heart, BBQ, and clinical practitioners as neologists: Developing a lexicon for clinical practice and school/university partnerships. *School-University Partnerships, 12*(2), 62–72.

CHAPTER 3

How Black Colleges Can Recruit, Prepare, and Support Black Male Teachers

Verjanis Peoples and Ivory A. Toldson

The education system in the United States has an underrepresentation of Black male teachers. Researchers connect this underrepresentation to higher dropout rates among Black learners, racially discriminatory practices, disparities in school resource allocations, biases in hiring and placement, and racially biased assessments for teacher certification (Kelly & Torres Lugo, 2017). However, Black male teachers are a crucial part of the US education system (Toldson, 2019). Meaningful solutions are necessary to solve the absence of Black male teachers from primary, middle, and secondary schools across the nation. Historically Black colleges and universities (HBCUs) have demonstrated leadership in providing solutions to ensure more Black males have equitable opportunities to teach (Pearson, 2019). This chapter explains why Black male teachers are important for diverse school districts in the United States and how HBCUs can be used as a strategic resource to increase the number and capacity of Black male teachers. The chapter also highlights the findings of a program at Southern University, an HBCU in Baton Rouge, Louisiana, that supported Black male teachers.

1 The Shortage of Black Male Teachers

Today, of the more than six million teachers in the United States, nearly 80% are white, 9.6% are Black, 7.4% are Hispanic, 2.3% are Asian, and 1.2% are another race (Toldson, 2019). Eighty percent of all teachers are female. Relative to the composition of P-12 students in the United States, the current teaching force lacks racial and gender diversity. Black men represent less than 2% of the teaching force of a student body that is 7% Black male. By comparison, white female teachers comprise 63% of the teaching force of a student body that is 27% white female (Toldson, 2019). Some school advocates suspect that teachers who lack cultural proficiency may relate to Black and Hispanic students in a manner that undermines their potential.

Common conjecture links the shortage of Black males in the teaching profession to negative experiences that Black males have in PK–12 education, making them unlikely to select teaching as a career. However, these explanations and narratives regarding Black male teachers rely on stereotyping and supposition, which do not necessarily hold under a thorough analysis of collected data (Toldson, 2019). While Black males experience pervasive discrimination in grade school, teaching is the number one profession among Black males who have at least a bachelor's degree. Notwithstanding, the underrepresentation of Black male teachers connects more broadly to the societal problems within the Black community, including discriminatory hiring practices and inadequate educational accommodations for Black people generally. There is thus a symbiotic relationship between solving problems in the Black community and increasing the number and capacity of Black male teachers.

Louisiana has an insufficient number of Black male teachers, which explains its demand for more of them. There are 770,000 public school students in the state, and 309,000 of those are learners of color. However, there are 2,419 Black male teachers, and this ratio to that of students is approximately 0.78%. In terms of gender, male teachers of color constitute 13% of the workforce while their female counterparts are 18% of the teacher population (Lewis & Toldson, 2013). The statistics mirror national-level data, where Black male teachers form an insignificant portion of the teacher count.

The rate of teacher turnover constitutes another potential indicator of the shortage of male teachers of color in Louisiana and nationally. Male minority instructors quit the profession at a higher rate than white male educators, which has led to the falling number of Black male teachers (Ingersoll & May, 2011). Numerous reasons underlie this trend and may include perceived racism and other personal decisions. Regardless of the causes of Black male teacher turnover, current circumstances have led to fewer of these professionals in the education sector.

2 Why Black Male Teachers Are Important

Before a school district starts any efforts to recruit and retain Black male teachers, they should answer the following questions:
– *What kind of Black male teachers do you want?* Do you want Black male teachers with similar backgrounds, preparation and perspectives as most of your white teachers? Or are you looking for someone with a more diverse background who will challenge existing racially biased views and attitudes at the school?
– *Why do you want more Black male teachers?* Do you want Black male teachers to give relief from students you don't like teaching? Or do you want Black

male teachers as a professional resource to help all teachers (regardless of race or gender) and teach all students (regardless of race or gender)?
- *What is the role of Black male teachers?* Do you see Black male teachers as overseers and disciplinarians who can keep Black male students in line? Or as role models and trailblazers that can help Black male students dream bigger?
- *Why are Black male teachers important?* Do you want Black male teachers to play the role of a surrogate father to "troubled" fatherless Black students? Or play the role of a surrogate school administrator for ineffective and racially biased schools? (Toldson, 2019, pp. 76–77)

Black male teachers can be a professional resource to help other teachers understand race, racism, and privilege in the classroom, to improve the learning environment for all students. Research suggests that persons of a privileged social group need to make conscious adjustments to develop authentic relationships with less privileged groups (Ullucci, 2011). Standard rubrics of evaluating teachers, such as knowledge, pedagogy and organization, are insufficient because they do not account for the vast diversity in the classroom or the sociocultural context of education (Nieto, 2006). Therefore, the teaching force, which is approximately 80% white, needs greater diversity to help teachers to cultivate empathy and respect for students of different racialized identities (Houser, 2008; Marx & Pray, 2011). Empathy, moral and spiritual values, and self-interest are three factors that motivate people from privileged social groups to promote equity in the classroom (Goodman, 2000). Exposing educators to diverse cultures is an important strategy to increase their cultural awareness and empathy toward racially different students.

Improving teacher efficacy and teacher-student dialogue and aligning their mutual understanding of school rules showed effectiveness (Pas, Bradshaw, Hershfeldt, & Leaf, 2010; Thompson & Webber, 2010). "Whole-school" interventions that focus on schoolwide improvements in instructional methods, positive reinforcement, such as teacher "praise notes" (Nelson, Young, Young, & Cox, 2010), behavioral modeling, and data-based evaluation, have also demonstrated effectiveness (Bohanon et al., 2006; Lassen, Steele, & Sailor, 2006; Luiselli, Putnam, Handler, & Feinberg, 2005). Resilience and skill building among students also reduced behavioral problems and subsequent disciplinary referrals among students (Wyman et al., 2010). Attention to students' mental health may also reduce suspensions and disciplinary referrals among Black male students (Caldwell, Sewell, Parks, & Toldson, 2009).

A relationship between respect and academic success for Black males was found through analyzing three national surveys (Toldson, 2008). High-achieving

Black male students reported that their teachers were interested in them "as a person," treated them fairly, encouraged them to express their views and gave extra help when needed. Teachers who were deemed effective also routinely let their students know when they did a good job. Overall, Black male students who were successful perceived their teachers to be respectful people who treated them like they mattered and nurturing people who built up the students' strengths instead of making them "feel bad" about their weaknesses.

Toldson (2011) found that schools with more gang activity had lower overall levels of academic achievement among students. Students in schools with gang activity were also more likely to report being distracted from doing schoolwork because of other students misbehaving. These findings collectively suggest that teachers and administrators in schools with more gang activity are perceived by students to spend more time confronting problematic students, which may compromise the academic priorities of the school. Students in schools with less gang activity are more likely to report that teachers care about students, treat students with respect, spend less time punishing students, and are less likely to report that teachers do or say things that make students feel badly about themselves (Toldson, 2011).

Black students are significantly more likely to experience disillusionment with their teachers (Lewis, James, Hancock, & Hill-Jackson, 2008). Many teachers, particularly teachers in urban school districts, may become disenchanted because they feel they have little control over the conditions and circumstances that weaken student achievement (Toldson, 2011). Therefore, Black male teachers do not need to be disciplinarians to help Black students survive tough learning environments. They need to provide empathy and compassion to students, along with professional guidance and support to other teachers.

3   Recruiting Black Male Teachers

The United States Secretary of Education launched a national campaign in 2011 to encourage Black males to enter teaching. The campaign's goal was to ensure that by 2015, at least 80,000 Black male teachers had been recruited into education (Henry, 2017). The campaign was reinforced by the idea that if students encounter teachers from diverse cultures, they could expand their knowledge.

Some of the programs initiated in universities include Black Men Teach (BMT), founded in 2012, whose mission was to ensure increased recruitment of African American men in the American teacher-education program (Okezie, Alhamisi, & Glimps, 2016). The main program's goal was to ensure that Black male students became fully exposed to the education career through the guidance and counseling programs that constitute the high school courses.

Another recruiting program is Call Me MISTER (Mentors Instructing Students Towards Effective Role Models). The program aims to provide mentoring and effective role modeling for students. The initiative, which is based at Clemson University and has partnerships with twenty-five universities and colleges, has a role in ensuring an increase in educators from more diverse regions into the teaching field. The program focuses on students from underprivileged backgrounds in the low-performing schools to recruit them into teaching. The package also provides tuition courses to their recruits in the education field to ensure that they attain teacher diversity (Hill-Carter, 2013). Its team offers social, cultural, and academic purposes for its students and assistance programs in placement, thereby encouraging individuals from diverse origins to join.

The US Department of Defense sponsors another Troops to Teachers (TTT) program. This program's role is mainly to initiate individuals' transition, mostly African American persons, from the military into the education sector. The program offers full sponsorship to people who are willing to divert their career into education, attracting more individuals into that field.

4 The Importance of Historically Black Colleges and Universities (HBCUs) to Primary and Secondary Education

HBCUs have played a prominent role in advancing of Black social progress and racial conciliation in higher education in the United States, as well as in the lives of individual Americans. HBCUs have used education as a vehicle for fighting against racial bias, discrimination, and oppression (Crewe, 2017). Serving as the "pipeline" to education for people who gained freedom from slavery, HBCUs had a three-dimensional function (Stevenson, 2007, p. 99): First, to promote civil rights; second, to improve Black people's opportunities in the post-slavery period; and third, to offer the same possibilities to Black students as to their white peers. It is impossible to overestimate the role of HBCUs in the establishment of Black people's intellectual, cultural, and spiritual development.

Since their foundation, HBCUs have faced various levels of demand and have served different purposes depending on the prevailing social issues in the nation. However, an undoubted fact about HBCUs is that they have always pursued the noble mission of making the lives of young Black Americans richer in terms of opportunities they receive and the knowledge they gain. During the periods of reconstruction and post-reconstruction, as newly emancipated Black people endeavored to obtain legal recognition as US citizens, the first HBCUs emerged and developed their agendas.

At the same time, they had to resist the terroristic actions of hostile white southerners. Since their inception, HBCUs have lacked both the legal and financial support to be competitive. One of the greatest developments occurred in 1862 with the implementation of the first *Morrill Land Grant Act* (Harper, Patton, & Wooden, 2009). With the help of the Act, it became possible to initiate educational movement in the spheres of mechanical arts and agriculture. The new law promoted the development of areas that had not received sufficient attention earlier. Despite the considerable gains made through the first Act, it was the second *Morrill Act* of 1890 that endowed equal funds for Black universities and colleges in seventeen states.

Although the Act's purpose was beneficial, educational facilities did not receive the promised funds. As a result, instead of focusing on agricultural and mechanical arts, many HBCUs concentrated on training Black students to become teachers. Since many graduates of facilities based on the 1890 Act became teachers, there turned out to be more qualified high school educators. As a result, more African American parents chose to send their children to school, which in turn fostered a new generation of students (Craig, 1992). Further, the general development of educational equality gave way to the establishment of more HBCUs.

Today, HBCUs demonstrate leadership in recruiting and preparing Black male teachers by advocating for educational policies that are race-conscious, instead of race-neutral, to expand Black students' educational opportunities. Reformulating these policies requires HBCUs to have a measure of autonomy to advance curricula that uphold social justice in education (Sanders, 2020). HBCUs need to increase opportunities for Black teachers to incorporate cultural experience and knowledge in schools. Since African American students face the worst forms of inequities the school system, future teachers of color need to use innovative educational strategies that combine pedagogy and policy advocacy (Pearson, 2019). According to Pearson, HBCU teacher preparation programs have three primary roles: reforming programs for teachers' pre-service education; recommending inclusive poverty analyses; and adding investigative connectivity between poverty and race to teacher preparation programs.

5 State Higher Education Executive Officers (SHEEO) Project Pipeline Repair Case Study

The State Higher Education Executive Officers Association (SHEEO), the Louisiana Board of Regents and the School of Education at Southern University and A&M College planned, implemented, and evaluated Project Pipeline Repair: Restoring Minority Male Participation and Persistence in Teacher Education Programs. The purpose of the project was to increase the number of highly competent minority male teachers to teach in underserved elementary school systems in Louisiana.

Key project features included the early enrollment of prospective educators as students during their junior year of high school, formative and summative performance assessments, individualized intervention strategies to close ACT achievement gaps, supplemental self-paced learning platforms, personal laptops, uniforms, on-campus summer residency, mentoring and academic advising, social events, and completion of college credits for teacher education programs through dual enrollment prior to admittance in college. Participants achieved expected outcomes through emphasizing the development of written and oral communication skills, critical thinking, teamwork, and quantitative literacy. Besides closing academic achievement gaps, the project aimed to build a sound foundation for participants to develop the requisite desire, knowledge, skills, and dispositions of highly competent and effective educators.

Dr. Verjanis Peoples served as the project director and is the director of the School of Education at Southern University and A&M College. As a seasoned educator, she offered leadership in strategies that impacted the success of the program. The three-year Project Pipeline Repair Program was implemented in Louisiana, Mississippi, and South Carolina. The participating HBCUs were the University of Arkansas at Pine Bluff, Southern University and A&M College in Baton Rouge, Alcorn State University, and Claflin University. Each university was charged with recruiting ten to twelve minority male high school students in the tenth grade to participate in each program. The Project Pipeline Repair outcomes for the thirty to thirty-five minority male participants enrolled in the program included their successful program completion, academic improvement, and a shift in their understanding of the teaching profession.

In Louisiana, from among the high schools that were selected by the School of Education at Southern University and A&M College, ten minority males were recruited to participate in the project. The tenth graders had a 2.5 GPA and had expressed keen interest in becoming a teacher. The project was initiated by the State of Louisiana in a special event with the commissioner of higher education and by the university, with an opportunity to introduce the young men to the University Board of Supervisors. These students were actively involved in the project throughout their sophomore, junior, and senior years. A special graduation ceremony was held at the end of their senior year by the School of Education to celebrate their successful completion of the three-year program.

The project recognized that the mentoring was an effective and important aspect of the program. Each participant was assigned a male college professor, who was trained as a mentor for the program and served as a role model, resource, and professional contact. Throughout the program, mentors and mentees met once a week to discuss issues related to the students' academic and personal affairs as well as other issues. Mentors used the information gathered through these meetings to inform the project about the needs of students. In addition, mentors and mentees joined together to attend sports events, social and religious gatherings, and other activities in which participants were involved.

At the conclusion of the Project Pipeline Repair, six of the ten minority male participants enrolled in the School of Education at Southern University and A&M College as a result of the project. This increase in the number of Black males entering the School of Education demonstrated that the program had effectively provided a pipeline from high school to college that increased the number of minority male students entering the teaching profession. This pipeline required the building of a support network to guide the students through so that candidates were prepared to enter the teaching profession. Southern University's School of Education continues to mentor minority male teacher candidates in an effort to retain the candidates throughout their matriculation in teacher education programs.

6   Summary of the Program

6.1   *The Shortage of Black Male Educators*
As mentioned, Black males only comprise 2% of teachers in the US education system. The reasons for this shortage are associated with negative experiences for them, such as racial discrimination. Similarly, suspensions and high dropout rates contribute to the shortages because the majority of them fail to graduate. The failure to diversify the US education system contributes to their low numbers. The discrepancies arising from selection bias and systemic discrimination lock them out of teaching careers. Lastly, the lack of essential policies to foresee their inclusion in the teaching profession hinders their study pursuits.

6.2   *Importance of Black Male Teachers*
Black male teachers are often role models in their community and locality, undertaking their roles effectively as stipulated by their jurisdiction. The vast majority treat students with dignity despite facing their own challenges, and they refrain from holding prejudicial low expectations. They are crucially positioned to nurture, encourage, and have compassion with Black students while design instructional methods to suit the needs of all students.

6.3 *Importance of HBCUs to Primary and Secondary Education*

HBCUs are vital to primary and secondary education since they aim to increase the number of minority underrepresented groups. Similarly, they train and equip teachers with relevant skills for their profession. In addition, they can facilitate partnership programs and continuity in the advancement of educational professionalism. HBCUs furthermore set benchmarks to ensure competition and create a compromise using standardized exams to avoid eliminating particular groups (Sanders, 2020). HBCUs generate support for the education system from external sources and provide teachers with the freedom to choose what suits their students. While employing the necessary performance requirements, they also adjust teachers' preparation programs to increase workforce diversity.

6.4 *Critical Undertakings from the Case Study*

Reformulating policies to make them race-conscious is necessary to increase opportunities for Black male teachers and to diversify the teaching workforce. Altering the education system to accommodate and recruit more Black students is likewise crucial, including policy reformulation on matters relating to discipline, racial disparities and unequal opportunities, and evaluating the specific problems they face.

7 Conclusion

As outlined in this chapter, the United States is experiencing a shortage of Black male teachers. This shortage has been linked to biased suspensions, bad policies in the selection and placement of teachers, and racial disparities affecting payment and resource allocation. Despite all of this, they possess a vital perspective on society and could make valuable contributions.

HBCUs play essential role in both primary and secondary education systems since they seek to eliminate racial discrimination and disparities emanating within the US system (Sanders, 2020). In doing so, they create equal opportunities for all students to access quality education and be supplemented with the necessary resources for choosing and completing their desired courses (Ingersoll, May, & Collins, 2019). Similarly, they assist in eradicating obstacles that arise when Black students are seeking employment. HBCUs are geared towards increasing the number of Black male educators, who may have faced challenges and experiences that forced them to shelve their ambitions to study (Bristol & Goings, 2018). HBCUs further focus on other aspects that may be underlying the learning process as they seek to understand and remedy the dearth of Black male educators.

Ensuring that as many Black teachers are engaged in the US education system as possible requires evaluating all factors tied to teaching. These factors will be necessary to determine and formulate the best solutions for eradicating the obvious disparities and discrimination against Blacks. Teaching requires understanding the needs and requirements of every learner. It further requires treating students, regardless of their race, with dignity, respect, compassion, and care.

References

Bohanon, H., Fenning, P., Carney, K. L., Minnis-Kim, M. J., Anderson-Harriss, S., Moroz, K. B. (2006). Schoolwide application of positive behavior support in an urban high school. *Journal of Positive Behavior Interventions, 8*(3), 131–145.

Bristol, T. J., & Goings, R. B. (2018). Exploring the boundary-heightening experiences of Black male teachers: Lessons for teacher education programs. *Journal of Teacher Education, 70*(1), 51–64. https://doi.org/10.1177/0022487118789367

Caldwell, L. D., Sewell, A. A., Parks, N., & Toldson, I. A. (2009). Guest editorial: Before the bell rings: Implementing coordinated school health models to influence the academic achievement of African American males. *Journal of Negro Education, 78*(3), 204–215.

Craig, L. A. (1992). "Raising among themselves": Black educational advancement and the Morrill act of 1890. *Agriculture and Human Values, 9*(1), 31–37.

Crewe, S. E. (2017). Education with intent – The HBCU experience. *Journal of Human Behavior in the Social Environment, 27*(5), 360–366. doi:10.1080/10911359.2017.1318622

Goodman, D. J. (2000). Motivating people from privileged groups to support social justice. *Teachers College Record, 102*(6), 1061.

Harper, S. R., Patton, L. D., & Wooden, O. A. (2009). Access and equity for African American students in higher education: A critical race historical analysis of policy efforts. *Journal of Higher Education, 80*(4), 389–414.

Henry, D. D. (2017). *Effective strategies for recruiting African American males into undergraduate teacher-education programs* [Doctoral dissertation]. Johnson & Wales University.

Hill-Carter, C. (2013). No one told us: Recruiting and retaining African American males in the college of education program from the urban and rural areas. In C. W. Lewis & I. A. Toldson (Eds.), *Black male teachers*. Emerald Group Publishing Limited.

Houser, N. O. (2008). Cultural plunge: A critical approach for multicultural development in teacher education. *Race, Ethnicity and Education, 11*(4), 465–482.

Ingersoll, R., & May, H. (2011). *Recruitment, retention, and the minority teacher shortage*. Consortium for Policy Research in Education, University of Pennsylvania and

Center for Educational Research in the Interest of Underserved Students, University of California, Santa Cruz.

Ingersoll, R., May, H., & Collins, G. (2019). Recruitment, employment, retention and the minority teacher shortage. *Education Policy Analysis Archives*, *27*, 37. https://doi.org/10.14507/epaa.27.3714

Kelly, P., & Torres Lugo, S. (2017). The imperative of closing racial and ethnic gaps in college attainment. *Change: The Magazine of Higher Learning*, *49*(5), 46–49. https://doi.org/10.1080/00091383.2017.1366811

Lassen, S. R., Steele, M. M., & Sailor, W. (2006). The relationship of school-wide positive behavior Support to academic achievement in an urban middle school. *Psychology in the Schools*, *43*(6), 701–712.

Lewis, C., & Toldson, I. A. (Eds.). (2013). *Black male teachers: Diversifying the United States' teacher workforce*. Emerald Group Publishing Limited.

Lewis, C. W., James, M., Hancock, S., & Hill-Jackson, V. (2008). Framing African American students' success and failure in urban settings. *Urban Education*, *43*(2), 127–153.

Luiselli, J. K., Putnam, R. F., Handler, M. W., & Feinberg, A. B. (2005). Whole-school positive behaviour support: Effects on student discipline problems and academic performance. *Educational Psychology*, *25*(2/3), 183–198.

Marx, S., & Pray, L. (2011). Living and learning in Mexico: Developing empathy for English language learners through study abroad. *Race, Ethnicity and Education*, *14*(4), 507–535.

Nelson, J. A. P., Young, B. J., Young, E. L., & Cox, G. (2010). Using teacher-written praise notes to promote a positive environment in a middle school. *Preventing School Failure*, *54*(2), 119–125.

Nieto, S. (2006). Solidarity, courage and heart: What teacher educators can learn from a new generation of teachers. *Intercultural Education*, *17*(5), 457–473.

Okezie, C. E., Alhamisi, J., & Glimps, B. J. (2016). The promise for African American male students in teacher education at Marygrove College. In *Gender and diversity issues in religious-based institutions and organizations* (pp. 137–158). IGI Global.

Pas, E. T., Bradshaw, C. P., Hershfeldt, P. A., & Leaf, P. J. (2010). A multilevel exploration of the influence of teacher efficacy and burnout on response to student problem behavior and school-based service use. *School Psychology Quarterly*, *25*(1), 13–27.

Pearson, D. (2019). Government intervention and educational equity: Leveraging educator preparation programmes at historically Black colleges and universities. In N. Karagiannis & J. E. King (Eds.), *A modern guide to state intervention* (pp. 276–296). https://doi.org/10.4337/9781789905083.00024

Sanders, C. (2020). Historically Black colleges and universities in the United States. *African American Studies*. https://doi.org/10.1093/obo/9780190280024-0088

Stevenson, J. M. (2007). From founding purpose to future positioning: Why historically Black colleges and universities must maintain but modify mission. *Jackson State University Researcher*, *21*(3), 99–102.

Toldson, I. A. (2008). *Breaking barriers: Plotting the path to academic success for school-age African-American males*. Congressional Black Caucus Foundation, Inc.

Toldson, I. A. (2011). *Breaking barriers 2: Plotting the path away from juvenile detention and toward academic success for school-age African American males*. Congressional Black Caucus Foundation, Inc.

Toldson, I. A. (2019). *No BS (Bad stats): Black people need people who believe in Black people enough not to believe every bad thing they hear about Black people*. Brill.

Ullucci, K. (2011). Learning to see: The development of race and class consciousness in white teachers. *Race, Ethnicity and Education, 14*(4), 561–577.

Wyman, P. A., Cross, W., Brown, C. H., Qin, Y., Xin, T., & Eberly, S. (2010). Intervention to strengthen emotional self-regulation in children with emerging mental health problems: Proximal impact on school behavior. *Journal of Abnormal Child Psychology, 38*(5), 707–720.

CHAPTER 4

The Efficacy of Assessment Measures Used for Admission and Certification and Differential Impact on People of Color

Ivan W. Banks

This chapter argues that the prevailing assessment tools like the Praxis exam series, which have been commonly used nationwide for admission into teacher education programs, can adversely affect African Americans' admittance into those programs and, ultimately, their ability to acquire teacher certification. It illustrates how exams contribute to declining numbers of African Americans entering the teaching profession by not taking into account cultural factors and other societal and educational roadblocks to traditional preparation for testing success. The chapter also makes it apparent that programs, certifying bodies, and state education departments have not embraced any effort to explore alternative, culturally relevant assessment options seriously. What does not get argued here is that the assessments have no place or purpose in making decisions about pre-service or in-service teachers. The particular concern in this chapter is in the insufficient number of African Americans who enter and remain in the teaching profession. The reasoning behind this shortfall is related to the use of high-stakes assessments to admit or deny admission into teacher education programs. This factor is a specific concern for historically Black colleges and universities (HBCUs), as such practices represent obstacles to entries that place more emphasis on inputs, and they do not take into account the value-added dimensions of the more personalized and supportive environments that characterize HBCUs.

1 The Issue

Historically Black colleges and universities produce a disproportionately large number of African American teachers and public-school administrators and have some of the most respected teacher education programs in the country. Overwhelming research indicates that children of color need to see teachers, administrators, and other authority figures of color to be able to visualize and project themselves as accomplished leaders in their field (ETS, 2018). However, current assessment and certification tools, as well as national, state, and local practices, negatively impact the admission of African Americans into teacher education programs and subsequently reinforce the continued decline in the numbers of African Americans entering the teaching profession (ETS, 2018). This attribute is especially true for the Praxis exam series, which has been used nationally for admission into teacher education programs. The Educational Testing Service (2018, p. 4) reported that:

> The implications of better assessments for African American students is that the assessments would be better indicators of what students know and can do at all ability levels. They would better detect performance gaps when they exist; be more authentic, engaging, and accessible; and provide more diagnostic data to help teachers understand where learning support is needed.

Compared to the white students and the national average, African Americans fall behind in their median SAT scores by at least 100 aggregate points in both mathematics and English (Mercer, 1984). Therefore, the sole dependence on such tests threatens the future of their admissions into teacher education programs. The underrepresentation of African Americans in the teaching profession calls for the establishment of aggressive programs to contend for their increased recruitment. This nation must commit to closing the gap in minority entry into and continuity in the teaching profession to close the achievement gap of minority students. Such a strategy would guarantee that the capable and committed African Americans who aspire to be teachers but fail to get admission due to the prejudiced tests get their deserved chance. Teacher education programs need to acknowledge that society is multicultural and replicate this factor in the admission process to ensure that all racial groups are adequately represented (Mercer, 1984). It is essential to recognize the performance gaps between the white and African American students because of the historical inequalities in educational opportunities between the two groups, among other socioeconomic factors. This determinant will further drive the need for diversifying the assessment methods to capture the African Americans' academic abilities adequately by including factors like contextual elements in the recruitment of teacher education programs.

2   Culturally Appropriate and Culturally Relevant Measurement Options

The alternative, more culturally appropriate and relevant measurement options that may replace or advance the prevailing certification specifications can be formulated by analyzing the existing data on students' achievement and current assessment results (ETS, 2018). Such data must be extracted from large-scale evaluations because aggregate data can conceal the performance gap among student subgroups. The prevailing assessments, like the National Center for Education Statistics' PK–12 longitudinal, offer meaningful information about African American student performance, gender variations, and socioeconomic backgrounds; hence, it can be employed in formulating alternative assessments. This data analysis is necessary for the policymakers, teachers, and parents who are formulating educational prospects, creating syllabi and curricula, and guiding their children, respectively. According to Scott Marion, president and executive director of the Center for Assessment, the ideal alternatives should at least be essential, complex, authentic, equitable, instructional, rich, engaging, active, accessible, and feasible (ETS, 2018).

These characteristics suggest that the assessment should embody noble concepts and skills, strive for the extensive and meaningful engagement of students, remain within realistic bounds, and provide multiple means for diverse students to demonstrate their knowledge. Additionally, the assessment should let students collaborate with people and resources, accommodate students of various abilities, and be timely, affordable, and appropriate to the local context. Narrowing these traits into the African American scope means that the evaluations would indicate students' knowledge and skills as well as identify possible performance gaps by applying more advanced techniques, enhance authenticity, appeal, and accessibility, and provide more distinctive data to aid educators in discerning where learning assistance is necessary (ETS, 2018). This section discusses specific alternatives in the following subheadings to demonstrate the broad scope of options, to establish more agreeable and equitable assessments, and to have novel dimensions in the federal and state systems that apply to African Americans.

2.1   *Past Achievements*

Ranking students by their individual excellence is disadvantageous because it disregards the cultural aspects that influence academic performance. Tom Rudin, director of the Board on Higher Education and the Workforce at the National Academies of Sciences, Engineering, and Medicine, stated that "it is important for college admissions officers to look beyond individual attributes and accomplishments and consider the opportunities and obstacles students experience in the context of their communities, schools, and homes" (ETS, 2018, p. 5). The aforementioned directive calls for including past accomplishments because doing so eliminates the cultural prejudice within the current tests. This alternative was identified by the National Merit studies, which found no meaningful association between students' past accomplishments and their family backgrounds. Therefore, assessments should evaluate students' past achievements like first-year performance, leadership, and extracurricular activities, which are affected by students' household income. The principal advantage of this alternative is that it does not discriminate against underprivileged groups since varying income backgrounds among students do not realize a significant difference in the named accomplishments. SAT scores fail in this aspect because parental income has an impact on them – they more so represent students' socioeconomic background and not their potential achievements within and outside the classroom. Another benefit of this alternative method, as affirmed in previous research studies, is that it better foretells if students can complete their college and graduate school than SAT and other aptitude tests (Mercer, 1984).

2.2   Success Variables

African American students' success variables can get employed as alternative admittance standards. This was verified by research studies that investigated the similar and diverse traits of prosperous African Americans who were admitted to the University of Florida Expanded Educational Opportunities Program (EEOP) (Mercer, 1984). In this case, the established variables were timely goals, high school curriculum completion, motivation, study habits, extracurricular activities, perceptions and attitudes, and working hours. Upon determining the variables, the research advised that further studies need to elevate their significance and define an admission standard that will make them an appropriate alternative to conventional policies.

2.3   The Ford Foundation's Value-Added Model

The value-added alternative would base students' admission on their academic and growth potential and not their achievements on tests. The Ford Foundation proposed such a model and recommends that the examination review and grading incorporate periodic national and local assessments of students' development (Mercer, 1984). The model would completely replace the current measures because it would offer feedback that allows the relevant stakeholders to implement the necessary modifications to enhance education procedures. This approach would also provide data to evaluate current learning program efficiency. Additionally, it would support the inclusion of non-cognitive measures like interpersonal factors to expand competencies.

2.4   Mastery Model

The mastery model relies on the opinion that potential teachers need to have a specified aggregate of qualities that will make them competent educators.

These traits include leadership, sensitivity, oral and written communication, organization and planning, perception and analytical skills, decision making, flexibility, and adaptability (Mercer, 1984). In this model, the potential teacher should have leadership skills, which warrants that they can control situations and guide and coordinate others. The sensitivity quality means that they acknowledge interpersonal differences and are sympathetic to their students' requirements. The potential teacher also needs to have competent oral and written communication skills to guarantee that they can articulate their ideas clearly to other people. The organizing, planning, perception, and analytical skills will ensure that they can prioritize and organize tasks properly by structuring objectives, and they can identify the crucial elements of an event to distinguish problems, respectively. Decision making, flexibility, and adaptability guarantee that they can undertake a logical progression and change their standard courses based on current demanding situations. These characteristics need to have even influences on the admission methods, and they can be evaluated through a specified assessment station within a day after the corresponding tests (Mercer, 1984). Here, students interested in teacher education who score below the SAT 835 and ACT 17 need to complete the tests based on the listed competencies within two days. Failure to gain admittance will get succeeded by a report that identifies their paucities and recommends improvement areas, and they will get one more try on the same test after a year.

2.5 *Situational Judgment Inventory and Biodata*

The alternative of applying situational judgment inventory and biodata has been suggested by Neal Schmitt, an emeritus professor of psychology and management. Schmitt stated them as two proven non-cognitive augmented measures of predicting student performance. He built on these two alternatives by outlining twelve areas of student performance that got revealed in preceding studies (ETS, 2018). In his research, he concluded that the first three of these dimensions are intellectual. These factors are creative and cultural sensitivity, general knowledge and education, and perpetual learning, enthusiasm, and curiosity. The next three dimensions are interpersonal – that is, diversity sensitivity, interpersonal skills, and leadership. The last six are intrapersonal: citizenship and social responsibility, ethics, career introduction, well-being, perseverance and flexibility, and life skills. Such a distinction was essential to clarify the significance of non-cognitive determinants. Situational judgment inventory is a measure in which a circumstance gets exhibited with its various alternative plans. Hence, the examinee needs to confirm their most and least likely course of action. Biodata includes concise multiple-choice questions that can get compiled in a report about one's background and preferences.

These two non-cognitive measures are useful in the admission series to raise the number of African American student entries because they have group variations that are lower than those of the high school GPA, SAT, and ACT scores (ETS, 2018). Lower group distinctions are essential, since they will resolve the insensitivity in cultural issues in the assessments regarding HBCUs that negatively impact prospective African American teachers' entry to teacher education programs. For example, an HBCU like Florida A&M University that demonstrated a lower aggregate SAT and ACT score than predominantly white colleges and universities can now obtain another admission alternative for the teacher education curricula (Mercer, 1984). Generally, the situational judgment inventory and biodata are formative, task-based, and open-ended assessments that weigh non-cognitive abilities and diversity against the hurdles in educational outcome.

3 Conceptual Model

The conceptual model alternative was suggested by Greg Perfetto, a research scientist, after he re-examined the existing model of environmental context with data alignment, which includes neighborhood, family, and high school interactions (ETS, 2018). The neighborhood is an external context that incorporates socioeconomic aspects beyond the home, family and friends, as well as cultural factors like crime, poverty, occupancy levels, and housing value. The family covers culture and the education support system, familiarity with the admission methods, and financial limitations. These circumstances may include family income and parents' education level. The high school environment encompasses the culture of joining colleges that is within the school, as well as education-oriented support, resources, and counseling like curricula, free lunch services, and advance-placement opportunities. Perfetto developed these additional contexts by including adversity indices within the educational setting; this augmentation guarantees that the admission officers will comprehend respondents' obstacles, opportunities, and resources, among other environmental circumstances (ETS, 2018). It will also ensure that there is a methodical way of weighing and acknowledging students' experiences, and it will warrant that assessments are contextual enough to draw equity in education.

3.1 *Creating More Reliable and Impartial Assessments*

Equitable assessments are both fair and culturally relevant. Michael Walker, a research scientist on the College Board, recommended that the evaluation developers eliminate culturally biased areas and those drawing upon differential preparation by subgroups, including instead simple and challenging queries that most respondents would answer accurately or wrongly, respectively, to realize more equitable assessments. This approach also means that technological-based assessments need reviewing to guarantee that the differences in technological exposure are not a cause of heightened performance gaps. It would, for instance, further improve the 2015 Gallup polls, which discovered that only half of students found their academics engaging, which presents a crisis in which minority students and those from low-income households are unfairly targeted (ETS, 2018). Bringing about more equitable change means acknowledging punitive measures that cancel such things as art curricula and modifying school activities for students and parents. The resulting assessment after these changes should, therefore, extend learning opportunities, promote beneficial tracking, and discourage the closure of beneficial curricular elements. This will resolve the current assessment issue that encourages parents to have their children "opt-out" of taking standardized examinations, to express their misgivings about tests (ETS, 2018). The ultimate goal of equitable assessments is to eliminate African American students' exclusion and instead foster accessible educational opportunities.

4 Current Research That Validates the Study

Various research reinforces the hypothesis that students of color need to see and meaningfully interact with teachers and administrators of color to visualize and project themselves as accomplished leaders. However, some analysts have recorded that the racial balance among the teachers is extensively inconsistent with the current number of students in public schools (National Education Association, 2014, as cited in Lindsay & Hart, 2017). For example, Maxwell (2014) reported that in the fall of that year, students from minority races were the majority of those in public schools. In the same year, Boser (2014) cited that diversity among teachers had decreased. The same case has applied in public and high-poverty institutions that enlist large numbers of minority students, such that, although teachers of color should be the dominant teaching staff, white teachers are the majority by at least 65% (Ingersoll & May, 2011, as cited in Wright et al., 2017).

Previous studies have identified the link between teachers' racial identities and student performance, especially in environments that have high poverty levels (Ogbu, 1992, as cited in Goldhaber et al., 2019). They suggest that a teacher of the same race as the students will significantly impact students' achievement. Wright et al. (2017) found that matching teachers' and students' racial identities at the onset of education influences student behavior significantly, and the paper suggested that elementary institutions should formulate environments that maximize that advantage. Such implementation can eradicate the mismatch in externalizing behaviors, which heightens the probability of school success. Dee (2004, as cited in Goldhaber et al., 2019) analyzed scores from an experiment that randomly allocated students to teachers and affirmed that students who were taught by the teacher from their race totaled a 0.11 and 0.06 higher standard deviation in mathematics and reading, respectively, than those with a teacher from a different race. The study also identified that this impact was intensified in African American students versus students from other races.

Other research studies that have employed more extensive databases match these findings. These include Clotfelter et al. (2007, as cited in Goldhaber et al., 2019), who found that students with a teacher of the same race scored 0.03 and 0.02 higher standard deviations in test scores for mathematics and readings than those with a teacher of a different race. This dataset was used by Goldhaber and Hansen (2010, as cited in Goldhaber et al., 2019), who further confirmed the conclusion that these effects are more substantial in African American students since they scored 0.04 higher standard deviations than white students when they had a teacher of the same race than when they had a teacher of a different race. Egalite et al. (2015) replicated the consistency of these findings by getting 0.02 and 0.004 higher standard deviations in mathematics and reading for some African American student classrooms with teachers of the same race versus those with white teachers.

Some studies have linked the effects of having a teacher of the same race to outcomes like discipline, school dropout rates, and subjective assessments (Ehrenberg et al., 1995, as cited in Goldhaber et al., 2019). This association attests that a teacher of the same race as the student is more inclined to issue positive subjective assessments of future accomplishment and behavior than one of a different race. Gershenson et al. (2017, as cited in Goldhaber et al., 2019) deduced that an African American male student from a low-income household who gets at least one teacher of the same race between their third and fifth grade would increase their likelihood of pursuing a four-year degree course by 29% and reduce their chances of dropping out by 39%.

Dee (2005, as cited in Goldhaber et al., 2019) stated that a teacher of a different race increased the chances of evaluating a student of color as disruptive, inattentive, and lazy by 46%, 34%, and 28%, respectively. These findings demonstrate the significance of having teachers of the same race as the student because the subjective assessments by teacher that link to their race affect essential aspects like students' college recommendations. García (2015, as cited in Wright et al., 2017) ascertained that African American kindergarteners garnered lower ratings in self-control, learning strategies, and externalized behaviors than their white counterparts.

Some studies have linked that difference to the low numbers of minority teachers in the workforce, a situation that subjects a majority of the non-white and economically disadvantaged students to getting taught by Caucasian teachers (Downer et al., 2016). The labor statistics can attest to these findings because they report that white female teachers in early childhood education make up at least 75% of the workforce (National Research Council, 2012, as cited in Downer et al., 2016). This fact is critical, since such evaluations can affect future grades, among other outcomes. Therefore, various scholars have campaigned for educational system changes to evade such adverse effects.

The movement towards hiring more people of color in the teaching profession has become a top priority to ensure that students have teachers who look like them (Putman et al., 2016). This action for change was also supported by Richard Riley in 1998 when he was secretary of education, which proves that racial imbalance in teacher representation has existed for a long time (Goldhaber et al., 2019). The removal of this mismatch is specifically significant in the districts that have a large number of students of color. The first reason for supporting this campaign is that, although teachers may intend to do their best in their profession, they remain susceptible to the subconscious biases that they acquired from individual experiences with different races. As a result, their objective to assist all students equitably gets limited by their internalized prejudice.

When students have a teacher of their race, the teachers tend to more positively perceive their external behaviors and hold higher academic expectations than teachers of a different race (McGrady & Reynolds, 2012, as cited in Putman et al., 2016). A white teacher is likely to rate African American students more negatively than white students due to their misguided belief that the former have lower academic abilities. White teachers are also more inclined to discipline and suspend African American students for accounted misconduct (Skiba et al., 2002, as cited in Goldhaber et al., 2019). Lindsay and Hart (2017) reported that minority students receive disproportionately harsh disciplinary actions. In the same vein, Rudd (2014, as cited in Wright et al., 2017) stated that minority students get more severe punishment for the same offense as their white counterparts, and Noguera (2008) noted that this could originate from cultural misunderstandings that make white teachers perceive minority students as disruptive. This factor is critical, since disciplinary actions limit students' future accomplishments and behavior (Arcia, 2006, and Gregory &

Ripski, 2008, both as cited in Goldhaber et al., 2019). They also reinforce the school-to-prison pipeline, especially when punishment involves excluding students from the classroom (Lindsay & Hart, 2017).

Exclusionary discipline is equally responsible for achievement and behavioral gaps because it reduces the students' learning period (Morris & Perry, 2016, as cited in Lindsay & Hart, 2017). Such disciplinary actions by white teachers on African Americans get attributed to the aforementioned cultural disparities and negative stereotypes that occur when the teacher misinterprets students' behavior.

The second advantage of getting teachers who look like their students and share their backgrounds is that they are more efficient role models (Putman et al., 2016). When minority students have role models who are of a shared racialized identity, they understand that they can achieve academic success without having to act white (Fordham & Ogbu, 1986, as cited in Goldhaber et al., 2019). When they have a white teacher, who does not share a common cultural background with them, the teachers may fail to understand these students' cultures. For example, Morris (2005, as cited in Wright et al., 2017) found that predominantly white staffing supports Caucasian middle-class classroom behavior standards, and hence fails to acknowledge the language, social behavior, and cognitive abilities that minority students acquire from their cultures.

In this scenario, the cultural discontinuities make the students of color struggle to adjust to the academic and behavioral standards of the school. This issue is even visible among kindergarten children, who manifest notable achievement gaps early in their learning process (Downer et al., 2016). However, having teachers of the same race brings cultural harmony that improves performance because they can create a culturally appropriate learning strategy (Achinstein & Ogawa, 2011, and Ladson-Billings, 1992, both as cited in Wright et al., 2017). These educators also increase students' faith in education, give them hope for their future, attract positive perceptions about their teachers, and transform students' attitudes and behaviors. Interestingly, teachers who share the race as the students draw less absent days from students (Holt & Gershenson, 2015, as cited in Putman et al., 2016).

The third benefit of having teachers of the same race as their students is that it reduces cultural differences and ensures that teaching methods are more effective (Egalite et al., 2015, as cited in Putman et al., 2016). This circumstance has resulted in enhanced student performance in both mathematics and reading tests, especially for underachieving African American students. A teacher of the same race as the student will also tend to value the child's cultural assets, have positive relationships with their parents, offer classroom communication that relates to what students experience at home, and incorporate similar communication discourse (Nieto & Bode, 2008, as cited in Downer et al., 2016). Further studies attest that educators' friendliness, responsiveness, and consciousness towards the children in early childhood education is more positive when they share similar cultural backgrounds (Downer et al., 2016). Generally, research outcomes assert that racial matching of teachers and students encourages more desirable student performance than a mismatch.

The final advantage of having teachers who look like their student is that African American educators are more inclined to assign the African American students to gifted services than their colleagues from other races (Grissom & Redding, 2016, as cited in Putman et al., 2016). Increasing the number of Black teachers would thus resolve the notable underrepresentation of African Americans in gifted programs compared to their white companions. Grissom et al. (2017) cited the elementary schools' national sample, which ascertains that schools with more African American administrators had larger numbers of African American students in gifted services. Teachers of color also have a greater tendency to discourage assessment methods like IQ tests, which disadvantage students of color, and suggest appropriate changes or the inclusion of diverse evaluations of giftedness that enhance the possibility of identifying such qualities among minority students (Grissom et al., 2017).

In support of this stance, McBee (2006, as cited in Grissom et al., 2017) confirmed that enrollment into gifted services commences from evaluations by classroom teachers based on their opinions of students. Teachers of color are likely more aware of giftedness among minority students because they possess more cultural sensitivity, which eliminates the disadvantage of more so perceiving white students' giftedness than minority students even when they have comparable testimonies (Elhoweris et al., 2005, as cited in Grissom et al., 2017). Similarly, minority students' parents feel more inclined to approach teachers of a shared race to discuss their children's evaluation for gifted programs. These findings indicate that there is a strong association between teachers' ethnicity and the enrolling of students of color in gifted programs.

5   Case Study: HBCU s' Roles in Preparing Teacher Education Candidates

Anecdotally, the author is aware of one rural, high-minority district that employed forty teacher education program graduates. While some had master's degrees, the overwhelming majority of them were African American and working as teacher assistants simply because they could not pass the Praxis exam. The district took measures to engage a local HBCU to provide training on content and test-taking skills. Most of these persons were highly qualified professionals who would be good teachers and role models for children when student learning outcomes were taken into consideration. The following section discusses how HBCUs play a role in addressing these issues.

HBCUs have a role in preparing teacher education applicants for their entry to and retention in the teaching profession. Freeman (2001, as cited in Irvine & Fenwick, 2011) stated that at least half of African American teachers in various states like Missouri and Alabama get trained at HBCUs, and these institutions are solely responsible for the high numbers of educators in local districts. They also result in a diversified teaching workforce because they produce measurable numbers of African American teachers (Irvine & Fenwick, 2011). This quality is a significant advantage to high-poverty urban schools since African American teachers stay in the teaching profession longer than their white colleagues, who are likely to leave after the low-income African American students' population increases. This fact may be because teachers of color have a higher motivation in their teaching to collaborate with minority students to enhance their performance and lives, and they also view it as a way of giving back to society (Irvine & Fenwick, 2011). In the case of teachers' turnover, Ingersoll (2004, as cited in Irvine & Fenwick, 2011) reported that the abandonment of the teaching profession is at 33% and 46% for the first three and five years of new teachers' practice, respectively. These turnover values are 70% higher in high-poverty versus low-poverty schools (Irvine & Fenwick, 2011). A report by ETS (2007, as cited in Irvine & Fenwick, 2011) found that 52% of African American eighth graders got abandoned by at least one teacher before the end of the year while the same case was 28% for white students. Therefore, HBCUs' effort in preparing teacher education candidates for entry into and success in the teaching profession is significant because a high African American teacher availability can relieve the critical teachers' deficit for high-needs schools.

HBCUs' first specific function in preparing and retaining teachers of color in their profession is to support innovative, research-based teacher education programs (Irvine & Fenwick, 2011). In this, they have spurred tangible reforms that generate national policy. They also aid in forming alternative measures of preparing and assessing students so that outcomes reflect enhanced, context-specific designs. HBCUs' second value in preparing and retaining potential teachers is that they invest in middle and high school teacher recruitment efforts that enroll students of color in significant numbers (Irvine & Fenwick, 2011). This approach guarantees that students gain interest in the profession from timely exposure that they acquire via prospective teacher-magnet programs and clubs.

HBCUs' third strategy in this mission is to employ both conventional and alternative methods of recruitment and assessment in teacher education programs (Irvine & Fenwick, 2011). Traditional assessment modes remain included because assessment content can be used to determine the knowledge and skills that students possess (Stecher, 2014). This fact is more accurate for multiple-choice questions that produce more specific results, but they have the shortcoming of limiting the deduction of the students' comprehension of a specified subject. Another disadvantage of multiple-choice questions is that they have inadequate approximations when it comes to assessing behaviors like forming analyses and writing essays (Stecher, 2014). These multiple-choice examination weaknesses also trickle into the tested aspects because their format limits the evaluation of desired skills. Therefore, conventional evaluations support the use of performance assessments to extend the former estimations' range. Performance assessments can collect more fulsome and constructive responses by applying open-ended questions to maintain an authenticity regarding real-life events and thus reveal the overall cognitive abilities of a student (Stecher, 2014). Alternative recruitment avenues include community colleges, PK–12 paraprofessionals, churches, civil rights organizations, childcare aides, and social services, among other community organizations. In community colleges, students of color can graduate and advance to four-year institutions (Irvine & Fenwick, 2011).

The fourth HBCU tactic could be to take advantage of their expertise by employing a unique design and establishing public schools within the campus (Ginsberg et al., 2017, as cited in James et al., 2020). This arrangement exists at Howard University, where it has the School for Mathematics and Science on campus. This institution ranks second among HBCUs as a fundamental research university based in Washington, DC (James et al., 2020). Their on-campus public school prepares students from middle schools to enroll in science, technology, engineering, and mathematics (STEM) careers by focusing on math and science syllabuses to ensure that the minority students gain entry into these fields. Here, educators from Howard University's teacher education program can get recruited to aid in the middle school students' learning. The on-campus public school also liaises with the university to establish research entities, support teaching professionals' instructional training, and employ the university's resources to provide polished learning experiences for the students (James et al., 2020). The program is consequently very attractive to minority teachers who can get direct assistance from the university in developing their careers while they gain experience in the field via the on-site urban school. Another HBCU that has employed the on-campus public school approach is Coppin State University. It has two of these institutions, which were formulated via the 2003 Coppin Urban Education Corridor to improve PK–12 students' accomplishments by preparing them via the use of quality education

(James et al., 2020). The on-premises Coppin Academy High School and Rosemont Elementary and Middle Schools in Baltimore, Maryland, boost the number of learners who are ready for higher learning and careers. Like the Howard University campus-based institution, these schools acquire their teachers from campus graduates, who make up over 30% of their teaching staff (Ginsberg et al., 2017, as cited in James et al., 2020).

HBCUs' fifth effort in this direction could be to expand their programs to diversify the teaching workforce further (James et al., 2020). For example, North Carolina A&T State University has implemented the 2+2 Transfer Program to establish a recruitment and preparation schedule for potential teachers of color, which allows their seamless transfer from the community colleges' two-year professions into the four-year degree courses (James et al., 2020). This policy grants students with associate degrees from community colleges the chance to gain admission in the North Carolina A&T State University to partake in their bachelor's in elementary education. The sixth HBCU approach involves collaborating with local schools to offer field experiences to their teaching candidates (James et al., 2020). For example, Coppin State University established its two on-campus schools by partnering with Baltimore's public schools, which led to strongly positive results for participating PK–12 students. James et al. (2020) reported that Coppin Academy High School had 87% timely graduation degrees between 2013 and 2014, and by 2017 and 2018, that value had reached 91%. The on-campus schools also had positive outcomes regarding safety and a sense of support and belonging, where 77% and 76% of students stated that they felt safe, integrated, and in touch, respectively, when they attended on-campus schools.

This report proves that HBCUs exist on the foundation of creating supportive atmospheres to enable the success of African American students (Arroyo & Gasman, 2014). These students get the opportunity to interact outside their classrooms with counselors, faculty members, and their peers. They also participate in extracurricular activities that motivate and empower them towards the pursuit of leadership. Generally, they get a sense of academic progress and accomplishment (Fleming 1984, as cited in Arroyo & Gasman, 2014). In areas where the reported support was not as high as expected, the records still deduced that the camaraderie, social networking, and interpersonal connections at HBCUs was greater than that in historically white institutions (HWI). This outcome is because HBCUs have individuals with shared cultures and racial identities that invoke feelings of well-being and encouragement among the students, even when other academic issues may drag them down.

HBCUs' final role in teacher education entry and success is that they encourage African American males' recruitment through programs that prepare them to become classroom teachers (Irvine & Fenwick, 2011). These institutions are part of the modern diversification approaches for African American male teachers that got highlighted in the African American recruitment policy for education reforms. Arne Duncan, former education secretary during Obama's administration, in fact targeted Black males to encourage them to enter teaching and remedy the severe P-12 gap (Underwood et al., 2019). This effort stimulated the expansion of several regional programs that have vied to establish alternative African American male recruiting strategies to address their underrepresentation in PK–12 schools. However, Howard University has been implementing this strategy for over twenty years by utilizing federal funds like the Ready to Teach program to diversify the teaching workforce via their insistence on recruiting African American males (Irvine & Fenwick, 2011). The university once attracted 363 aspirants for the twenty-five vacancies. Their model manifested the vast potential of African American male teachers' national recruitment, training, and employment in low-performing schools.

Generally, such policies will recruit, train, and place African American male teachers in high-poverty institutions. Such efforts make HBCUs' influence undeniable. While making up a small percentage of colleges and universities, HBCUs graduate 50% of African American teachers with bachelor's degrees (Underwood et al., 2019). Clemson University enacted the Call Me MISTER (Mentors Instructing Students Toward Effective Role Model) program to focus on connecting African American males who graduate from college with teaching positions in high-poverty elementary schools (Underwood et al., 2019). This program is part of the grow-your-own initiatives, which have the objectives of mentoring and preparing African American males for the teaching profession.

Alternative measures of short-term and long-term success may be fairer and more appropriate than those currently used. The first of such measures is the use of alternative teacher education programs (Irvine & Fenwick, 2011). These options would implement existing research, emphasizing opportunities for learners to strategize on, execute, and assess alternative teaching methods. They are a novel approach because, unlike other proposed alternatives, they shift the focus from the type of degree awarded, program terms, and sponsoring institution, among other structural concerns, whose research is inconclusive and often conflicting (Irvine & Fenwick, 2011). Alternative teacher education programs call for the review of contextual matters like curricula and social and institutional context, which HBCUs are primed for investigating.

The second measure involves using alternative assessments that correct the existing racially prejudiced evaluations (Irvine & Fenwick, 2011). This strategy would eradicate the cultural insensitivities that manifest in the entry pass rates on standardized examinations. The current programs are a significant hindrance to African Americans because their admission processes are limited to Praxis I tests (Irvine & Fenwick, 2011). These conventional examinations, which lead to licensing, favor white candidates, of which at least 80% are middle-class females (Evans & Leonard, 2013). This fact begs for analysis of diversity in the teaching profession because Praxis I seems to be the reason behind the shortfall in the admission of African American applicants. Eliminating entrance examinations in the initial screening will most likely resolve the issue of teacher shortages and enrollments, particularly given their inefficient prediction of the effectiveness and preparation of teacher education aspirants (Darling-Hammond, 2000, as cited in Evans & Leonard, 2013). Eradicating Praxis I will not dilute African American teachers' capability because they score higher than other candidates in the pedagogical, content, and communication skills assessment in the Praxis II examination (Irvine & Fenwick, 2011). Some teacher education programs grant licenses after they complete their bachelor's degree, while others only issue the license after graduation. HBCUs try to correct the low licensure rate among African Americans by extending examination preparation programs to increase their passing percentage (Evans & Leonard, 2013). Teacher education policymakers need to recognize the entry barriers for African Americans in the traditional programs, and HBCUs have made it their task to acknowledge and circumvent these hindrances by issuing supportive tutorials for the Praxis examinations, in cases where eliminating them have proven to be difficult, and offering financial aid in taking the tests (Evans & Leonard, 2013). They have modeled their environments to promote teacher retention.

The third measure of short and long-term success that might be fairer and more appropriate than those currently employed is the application of alternative certification programs. This approach will resolve the issue of teacher shortages among high-poverty schools in urban areas that have students of color as their majority attendees (Evans & Leonard, 2013). They will provide teachers with provisional certificates that grant them the mandate to teach in urban institutions as they work to obtain first certification and a master's degree. Alternative certifications may get viewed as quick fixes that only result in having unpolished classroom teachers. However, teachers in these circumstances have proven to develop gradually over the last three decades because they bring diversity in age and racial orientation to the teaching profession (Madkins, 2011, as cited in Evans & Leonard, 2013). These alternatives include Teach for America (TFA), New York City Teaching Fellows (NYCTF), and Tomorrow in Oakland (TTO), among which TTO has been more successful in diversifying teacher recruitments.

6 Enhanced Support of HBCUs by Certification and Accreditation Entities

In the past, national accreditation bodies like the National Council for Accreditation of Teacher Education (NCATE) and the Teacher Education Accreditation Council (TEAC) have grappled with issues of equity and inclusion when working with HBCUs (Kirby, 2006). In 2000, NCATE attempted to employ an evidence-based accreditation approach, but using standards from biased research can yield biased outcomes. Cultural considerations for information from internal performance data, certification examinations, and external field practice is necessary for evaluating HBCU teacher preparation programs. NCATE, TEAC, and subsequent accreditation bodies recognized the necessity of evidence on unit assessments that record and analyze data to guide in enhancing the teacher education programs (Kirby et al., 2006), but more work is necessary to develop genuinely inclusive accreditation standards. Culturally competent accreditation requires multiple culturally fair assessments, diverse accreditation committees, and embedded procedures to assess biases.

HBCUs should get enhanced support from certification and accreditation bodies to aid in their preparation of teacher education candidates and policymakers should promote culturally fair national accreditation and evaluation of teacher education programs at HBCUs (Irvine & Fenwick, 2011). These supports include internal and regional assessments, where HBCUs can affirm if these examinations align with their mission and if they rely on reputable pedagogy, content knowledge, or both (Shulman, 1987, as cited in Irvine & Fenwick, 2011). Content knowledge is a corroborated fundamental requirement for teaching, and it has an indispensable status in teacher programs certification (Hill, 2007, as cited in Phelps et al., 2014). However, content knowledge alone does not give a teacher full proficiency in their classrooms. Shulman (1986, as cited in Phelps et al., 2014) discussed teachers' responsibilities in comprehending and applying the most relevant modes of ideas and examples such that they will be understood easily. In a rapidly diversifying nation, "relevant" acts in tandem with culture.

Culture influences education programs' content, students, curriculum, and teaching knowledge. Regarding students and content, educators must be familiar with misconceptions or complications that students may manifest. The curriculum and content involve an awareness of applying the current curricula in teaching exact content (Phelps et al., 2014). Specialized knowledge is also useful in teaching education since it prescribes that educators need to know multiple approaches to resolving one issue to meet varying student needs. Emerging research on content knowledge theory is beneficial to the teaching fraternity because they link the teaching workforce and the familiarity required to deliver the profession effectively (Phelps et al., 2014).

Therefore, assessments need to designate areas that measure the candidates' cultural content knowledge. These efforts will give HBCUs the resources they need to establish an assessment foundation, sustain a perpetual practice of reviewing and evaluating performance, and contract dedicated staff who support that purpose. Assistance from policymakers can expand teacher education programs at HBCUs and aid HBCUs in satisfying the accreditation criteria and tracking the preparation program results.

Another way by which HBCUs can get enhanced support from accreditation organizations to serve their preparation of teacher aspirants is through promoting collaborative institution-based programs that produce board-certified educators who are African American (Irvine & Fenwick, 2011). Previous research has verified that board-certified teachers were more useful to Hispanic and African American students than other learners (Cavalluzzo, 2004, as cited in Irvine & Fenwick, 2011) – however, despite this finding, the declared numbers of board-certified teachers were only 7,667 teachers of color out of 74,000, which reveals that more minority teachers are required.

Existing collaborative institution-based programs include the National Board for Professional Teaching Standards (NBPTS), which complements preparation, accreditation, licensing, and essential development. Irvine and Fenwick stated that "NBPTS is the greatest distinction for accomplished teachers in the United States" (2011, p. 204), and it has universally modeled standards and evaluations. They backed their deductions by citing a three-year assessment, which concluded that NBPTS embodies rigorous professional advancement and elevates student accomplishment and learning.

7 Conclusion

Concerns to diversify the teaching workforce have sparked a national conversation because the teaching profession is not as culturally representative as it should be. In this case, most citizens acknowledge that national dynamics are multicultural, and hence, they demand equal racial representation in every profession. A wide gap exists between the percentage of students versus teachers of color, and this factor causes a problem because teachers of color bring several advantages to minority students. These benefits include cultivating teacher-student trust since they offer more culturally relevant teaching, comprehending circumstances faced by students of color more precisely, and having more positive perceptions of students of color than their white colleagues.

The scarcity of teachers of color can be attributed to the disproportionality of suspending and expelling students of color, which eventually leads to academic withdrawal and enhances the possibility of future dropping out. The effects of this shortage even exist among kindergarten children, who fall behind by their third grade of study. The significant gap between the availability of teachers of color and the percentage of students of color exists because traditional assessment methods, like the Praxis exams, for enrolling in teacher education programs are culturally prejudiced.

Alternative assessments can successfully resolve these issues, and HBCUs are working to provide such techniques in various ways. These institutions have the principal goal of aiding in the teaching of African Americans, and they have upheld that aim by producing a notably high percentage of the African American teaching workforce. Another advantage lies in HBCUs' education delivery, such that minority students reported that they feel a firmer sense of support when they learn in these institutions than when they study in HWIs. Therefore, these institutions are worthy of the necessary support to gain accreditation for their teacher education programs so that they can continue to remedy the existing professional gap.

References

Arroyo, A., & Gasman, M. (2014). An HBCU-based educational approach for Black college student success: Toward a framework with implications for all institutions. *American Journal of Education, 121*(1), 57–85. http://dx.doi.org/10.1086/678112

Boser, U. (2014). *Teacher diversity revisited.* Center for American Progress. https://www.americanprogress.org/issues/race/reports/2014/05/04/88962/teacher-diversity-revised

Downer, J. T., Goble, P., Myers, S. S., & Pianta, R. C. (2016). Teacher-child racial/ethnic match within pre-kindergarten classrooms and children's early school adjustment. *Early Childhood Research Quarterly, 37,* 26–38. doi:10.1016/j.ecresq.2016.02.007

Egalite, A. J., Kisida, B., & Winters, M. A. (2015). Representation in the classroom: The effect of own-race teachers on student achievement. *Economics of Education Review, 45,* 44–52.

ETS. (2018). A focus on educational assessment: Advancing African-American education excellence. *Policy Evaluation & Research Center, 24*(2), 1–12. https://www.ets.org/Media/Research/pdf/PICPNV24N2.pdf

Evans, B. R., & Leonard, J. (2013). Recruiting and retaining Black teachers to work in urban schools. *SAGE Open, 3*(3), 215824401350298. doi: 10.1177/2158244013502989

Goldhaber, D., Theobald, R., & Tien, C. (2019). Why we need a diverse teacher workforce. *Phi Delta Kappan, 100*(5), 25–30. doi.org/10.1177%2F0031721719827540

Grissom, J. A., Rodriguez, L. A., & Kern, E. C. (2017). Teacher and principal diversity and the representation of students of color in gifted programs: Evidence from national data. *The Elementary School Journal, 117*(3), 396–422. doi:10.1086/690274

Irvine, J., & Fenwick, L. (2011). Teachers and teaching for the new millennium: The role of HBCUs. *The Journal of Negro Education, 80*(3), 197–208. doi: 10.2307/41341128.

James, W., Scott, L., & Temple, P. (2020). Strategies used by historically Black colleges and universities to recruit minority teacher education candidates. *Journal of the Association of Teacher Educators – Virginia, 13*, 76–104. https://static1.squarespace.com/static/5b2fca94f7939217ed700824/t/5e63b74f0a1d4b4e74ee41ca/1583593299299/TheTeacherEducators%27Journal_Spring_2020.pdf

Kirby, S. N., McCombs, J. S., Barney, H., & Naftel, S. (2006). Reforming teacher education: Something old, something new. *RAND*, 1–155. http://ays.issuelab.org/resources/10855/10855.pdf

Lindsay, C. A., & Hart, C. M. D. (2017). Exposure to same-race teachers and student disciplinary outcomes for Black students in North Carolina. *Educational Evaluation and Policy Analysis, 39*(3), 485–510. doi:10.3102/0162373717693109

Maxwell, L. A. (2014, 19 August). *US school enrollment hits majority-minority milestone*. Retrieved May 9, 2016, from http://www.edweek.org/ew/articles/2014/08/20/01demographics.h34.html

Mercer, W. A. (1984). Teacher education admission requirements: Alternatives for Black prospective teachers and other minorities. *Journal of Teacher Education, 35*(1), 26–29. doi:10.1177/002248718403500108

Noguera, P. (2008). *The trouble with Black boys and other reflections on race, equity, and the future of public education*. Wiley and Sons.

Phelps, G., Weren, B., Croft, A., & Gitomer, D. (2014). Developing content knowledge for teaching assessments for the measures of effective teaching study. *ETS Research Report Series*, 1–92. https://files.eric.ed.gov/fulltext/EJ1109301.pdf

Putman, H., Hansen, M., Walsh, K., & Quintero, D. (2016). *High hopes and harsh realities: The real challenges to building a diverse workforce*. Brown Center on Education Policy at Brookings. https://www.brookings.edu/wp-content/uploads/2016/08/browncenter_20160818_teacherdiversityreportpr_hansen.pdf

Stecher, B. (2014). Looking back: Performance assessment in an era of standards-based educational accountability. In L. Darling-Hammond & F. Adamson (Eds.), *Beyond the bubble test: How performance assessments support 21st century learning* (pp. 17–52). John Wiley & Sons, Inc.

Underwood, K., Smith, D., Lutz-Johnson, H., Taylor, J., & Roberts, M. (2019). *Having our say: Examining the career trajectories of Black male educators in P–12 education.* NNSTOY Partners. https://www.phoenix.edu/content/dam/uopx/doc/external/having-our-say.pdf

Wright, A., Gottfried, M. A., & Le, V.-N. (2017). A kindergarten teacher like me. *American Educational Research Journal, 54*(1 suppl), 78S–101S. doi:10.3102/0002831216635733

CHAPTER 5

Culturally Relevant Pedagogy
Decolonizing the Curriculum and Promoting Educational Equity

Anthony A. Pittman, Dywanna Smith, Delphia S. Smith and Demeturia Kelly

This chapter will provide the foundations of how culturally relevant pedagogy can be used as a tool to decolonize teacher education program curricula and promote educational equity. This study's main objective is to explore the literature and provide educators and administrators in educational institutions with critical information for shaping skills and dispositions to move current institutional practice towards instructions that are more culturally and linguistically diverse to accommodate the needs of underrepresented groups. Given the ongoing racial and social unrest in the US, and teachers are required to be equipped with knowledge that will help decolonize the curriculum. Educators require a deep understanding of instructional pedagogy that incorporates cultural diversity to stop systemic macroaggressions and create a feeling of belonging for PK–12 people of color. The advocacy for the fight against racism is lengthy in the United States and, still, much is to be done to attain educational equity.

The literature indicates that African American students are vulnerable, and their academic performance and educational engagement in higher education require more attention. There is systemic racism in institutions, and these margins can be important spaces for addressing this pervasive issue and ensuring that there is a transformation in education delivery. By leveraging marginalized students' lived experiences, this research provides recommendations for making policy changes, designing pedagogical practices, and instructional resources to foster humanizing and equitable classrooms. Teachers who specialize in asset-based pedagogies like culturally relevant pedagogy do not receive the appreciation and recognition they deserve. Teachers can be key pillars to addressing systemic racism by adopting culturally relevant pedagogy and understanding students' culture to encourage them to share their experiences within the learning context.

1   Introduction and Background

For many African Americans, discrimination and racism are facts of life (Meatto, 2019). Black Americans face overt and subtle discrimination from preschool to college, and their school performance can constrain many future opportunities. There are opportunity gaps in education, manifested in test score and grades. The opportunity gap does not only affect African Americans and their communities and families, but also the well-being of the entire nation. Present and past social and economic conditions are sources of the opportunity gaps (Bowman, Comer, & Johns, 2018). Societal efforts to eradicate the ill effects of discrimination and prejudice in schools for African Americans have not yet been fulfilled, as inequalities persist in the American education system (Peterson et al., 2016).

In the United States, racial segregation in public schools has been illegal for over sixty-five years. However, public schools remain significantly unequal and separate – with profound effects, particularly for Black students (Meatto, 2019). Racial segregation in public schools is problematic because racially segregated minority schools frequently have substantially fewer resources, thus employing less experienced teachers. Also, due to unequal educational resources, "neo-segregated" schools tend to have substandard facilities, fewer counseling services, larger class sizes, and lower per-student spending. Besides, there is a high likelihood that the neo-segregated schools will be surrounded by poor neighborhoods that have restricted access to community resources and with an increasingly high crime rate that hinders development and learning (Webb & Thomas, 2015).

According to Child Trends, educational expectations for Black children are lower as compared to their white peers. Additionally, compared to white peers, Black kids are more likely to be enrolled in low-quality schools (Cook, 2015). Like any other child, Black kids are born with the power to learn, but they need the experience to explore their potential fully. Capabilities develop via interactions with things and people that shape the brain's circuitry to control a kid's emotional, social, physical, and cognitive development. According to research findings, inborn drives to learn to propel some development aspects like using symbols, being sociable, and learning the language (Allen, 2019). Exposure to unloving adults, unreliable and inconsistent care, and extreme neglect and violence can be stressful for kids and stunt their developmental potential. To the contrary, supportive neighbors and friends, timely family treatment and counseling, understanding teachers, and/or therapeutic interventions can contribute towards stabilizing a kid's development as well as reducing stress (Rothstein, 2015).

2   Culturally Relevant Pedagogy

Howard and Rodriguez-Scheel (2017) defined culturally relevant pedagogy (CRP) as a method of teaching, whereby the instructors focus on individuals' culture and encourage the learners to relate the subject matter to their cultural experiences. This method is used in the United States to teach African American learners, and it has proved to be a significantly effective method of teaching students from diverse ethnicities. However, CRP is not relevant for ethnicities alone; it is also applied with communities such as LGBTQI. CRP also deals with the pedagogical aspect in which teachers impart cultural competence to learners.

Competence is seen in students as a result of student-based approaches to teaching and learning (Milner, 2017). Students' cultural strengths that are not common are identified and strengthened. Particularly, CRP provides a basis on which to foster academic well-being and learners' identities. Also, educators use their intellectual capabilities to help learners by imparting knowledge for these individuals to develop their full potential without considering their ethnic and racial backgrounds. Therefore, appropriate education structures and discrimination-free systems are developed to enhance this type of knowledge acquisition (Howard & Rodriguez-Scheel, 2017). CRP focuses on the success of the individual and the combined success of all students. It likewise enables teachers to link home and different school cultures while mobilizing students to be the medium of social change and also engaging them in learning activities.

3   Decolonizing the Curriculum

Decolonizing the curriculum means designing spaces and capital for a conversation among staff members on how to understand diverse cultures and understandings in the school curriculum (Jordan, 2016). Decolonization involves the process of going through the curriculum, removing some non-relevant written content, and replacing it with more relevant words. Further, to decolonize the curriculum entails coming up with resources and spaces for inclusive dialogue, where all participants of the school agree on how to cater to knowledge systems and all cultures concerning what is taught and its relevance to the learners' world. Curriculum development has been championed by various groups to advance towards decolonization in which people of color are more represented.

The Teaching Excellence Framework (TEF) and the National Student Survey had a key interest in recognizing students' voices regarding issues affecting them (Johnson et al., 2018). The institutions under TEF asked learners what their curriculum missed, and they reasoned together to advocate for developments. Such a process makes it easy for learners to understand a given concept because they are given the appropriate example that they can relate to from their cultural perspectives.

4   Educational Equity

Educational equity is the measure of fairness, inclusion, opportunity, and achievement in the education sector. It is the act of giving all learners the same opportunity, being fair to all of them, and encouraging them to achieve their goals. Fairness implies that personal interest in education should not hinder or interfere with each learners' academic success. Inclusion is a comprehensive standard that strives to involve everyone in the learning process. The two aspects advocate equal rights in education, including both gender and racial differences (Cahalan, Perna, Yamashita, Wright, & Santillan, 2018). Disabled students or others with special needs should be able to freely interact with typical students in the classrooms. The importance of educational equity is to enable all students to acquire knowledge and skills to help them productively engage in society. This will result in better social and economic conditions for individuals as well as the entire nation.

5   The Importance of Culturally Relevant Pedagogy

Culturally relevant pedagogy, decolonization of the curriculum, and educational equity are of prime importance in education today. CRP has greatly helped learners by supporting their culturally based strengths (Li & Carroll, 2017). Decolonization of the curriculum has facilitated the inclusion of learners' authentic worldviews instead of demeaning their culture by tacitly endorsing patriarchy and the normalization of whiteness. Educational equity strives to provide equal opportunities in education so that no learner experiences discrimination. One's culture and race are not determinants of opportunity in such a system. However, issues are not always as they seem since, in many cases, hidden forms of racism compromise educational equity.

Enacting CRP is not a simple task, and teachers face several challenges. Understanding it in the context of teaching requires some form of expertise. Allen (2019) noted that teachers' self-conception should inform their work and how they perceive others, their conceptions of knowledge, and their workplace social relationships. This study established that teaching is political and requires that teachers assist their students in critiquing societal systems. Allen observed that white teachers assumed the essence of critical consciousness when it came to CRP enactment. Therefore, Black teachers can similarly utilize such opportunities to re-assert and challenge deficient perspectives about Black students and adults. The research's overall argument highlighted the essence of how race works and impacts social institutions such as schools. Allen (2019) argued that Black teachers were receiving fewer considerations for promotion, particularly those who specialize in asset pedagogies like pedagogy dealing with culture.

6   The Intersection of Experiences and Identities

Understanding the intersection of experiences and identities is part of racial literacy that helps the learners understand how the educational system is compromised and biased to disadvantage students of color (Saavedra & Pérez, 2012). This means that the education system is set in a way that it subjugates those who are perceived as non-white. Through racial literacy, educators can deconstruct the white supremacy that dominates the education system and give the class a greater understanding of the experiences of students of color.

Behizadeh (2014) argues that students require more authentic writing choices. If the topics of classroom writing are severely limited, it blocks students from heartfelt expression. There is a connection between students' writing choice, expression, and, most importantly, impact. There are community issues that students may aim to communicate through their writing, and if this is allowed, this writing can be a release for students and also address certain aspects of society. One can argue that although issues of authenticity may be more evident among adolescents, an individual student's subjective take may vary because of their lived experiences and the genre in which they are composing – and, thus, more freedom must be given so that they can sufficiently express themselves.

Johnson and Bryan (2016) note that the murder of Black males in society has created new discourses in higher education spaces that all point to African-Americans' plight in the United States. The authors note that Black males have always been the target of white supremacy. Research has shown that violence against Black males results from a socially instilled view of race in which Black men are stereotyped. These biases normalize racialized violence against Black males, and to Johnson and Bryan (2016), this is their silent killer – it is only masked in other aspects of the society. The authors transfer the context of

Black males' misreading to the classroom to think about how these males are perceived in educational institutions and society writ large.

Society has repetitive narratives about Black males that portray them all as problematic and potential criminals. This is even evident in universities, and Johnson and Bryan (2016) noted that they operated in predominantly white universities. Therefore, they aimed to highlight social and equity issues at their workplace and the general issue of racism in higher education's pedagogical practices. They note that in PK–12 classrooms, 85% of educators are white, middle-class females who speak only one language but teach diverse groups of students from different ethnic, cultural, racial, and linguistic backgrounds.

This is a sensitive issue because it is difficult for the majority of educators to understand the plight of Black males and how marginalized they are. However, these educators would fail to develop culturally appropriate strategies to minimize Black males' distress in the learning environment. Not only did Johnson and Bryan (2016) note this, but Johnson, Bryan and Boutte (2018) furthermore explain that the PK–12 classroom is highly monopolized, and its structures reflect whiteness. This calls for educators to explore and understand the multiple layers of whiteness and how this can be used to propagate outdated models of criminalizing Black males through the education system. White female educators are perceived as a "white racial army" that uses various tactics to secure white supremacy.

The seriousness of having white educators as the majority in a racially diverse institution can only be understood through their role in the educational arena (Johnson, Bryan, & Boutte, 2018). Significantly, this group is responsible for teaching Black violence. While it would be unfair to blame all white educators, this nonetheless gives white supremacists fertile ground through which to propagate their stereotypes. Johnson and Bryan (2016) explain that white educators are strictly dedicated to respecting the white "Eurocentric Patriarchal Curriculum," which annihilates Black people and commits what Johnson and Bryan refer to as violent pedagogy. This curriculum is responsible for both the physical and spiritual death of Black and Brown learners (Dillard, 2012). Although these claims cannot be ascertained publicly, there is evidence that some people are dedicated to the continuity of white supremacy and but remain silent in the face of the media.

Schools generally value and privilege the Western culture of gaining Eurocentric knowledge while ignoring any cultural nuances or alternative approaches to gaining knowledge as practiced by people of color. This system engenders white supremacy and Black inferiority among students. Children are introduced to counterproductive views that end up fortifying the status quo. For instance, it leads to a policing system in which police see an eighteen-year-old

Black male as a miscreant, while politicians make laws that further the mass incarceration of Black men (Baker-Bell, 2020).

7 Microaggressions, Whiteness, and the Politics of Exclusion at the University

Normalized whiteness at colleges and universities creates education professionals who marginalize people of color in PK–12 education. To scholars like Sian (2019), there is a categorical coding in which universities are regarded as white spaces and in which the institutions are wired or organized on the basis of whiteness. This means that if you are non-white, you are required to conform to whiteness. Such institutionalized whiteness leads to a system in which racialized bodies experience discomfort and exposure as they feel that they do not belong there. Instead, they feel that they are vulnerable as nobody recognizes their culture. It should be noted that "whiteness" does not only refer to one's phenotypical traits or origin; it also refers to the complex structures of power, a form of entitlement, and a form of superior status. It reflects a social positioning in which those who belong there are racially and structurally privileged. Individuals who belong to this category or social positioning reap economic, social, and political benefits. From the perspective of whiteness, other racialized groups appear abnormal, invisible, and marginal.

Universities are one of the main sites where the hegemonic forms of racialization are reproduced and maintained by whiteness. Although universities are assumed to be spaces that support ideal representations of liberal bodies, the fact is there are serious racial tensions and the enactment of white supremacy presents itself under the guise of a liberal model. According to Sian (2019), most operations in the white academy do not direct confront racial issues. Confrontations are replaced by politics of exclusion in which bodies of color are firmly situated on the outside. Therefore, there are structural practices in a system, and they directly impact the prospects of Black people and other people of color. There are hidden racist practices, values, and organizational strategies that can be traced to white privilege. Institutional racism is manifested via everyday interactions and structural conditioning in which a racialized individual is intentionally or unintentionally subjected to hostile, derogatory, or negative microaggressions. Individuals who perpetrate these microaggressions are, in most cases, unaware that they are harming someone. As such, the microaggressions are subtle and confronting them may seem like pettiness because they are against the typical understanding of racism. As such, racial microaggressions are vague in nature, and this helps disguise racism in universities. Therefore, the highest chance is that where racism is not clear, and it is committed in a way that is not intentional, it is, in most cases, ignored (Sian, 2019).

Clearly, CRT is critical in society today because traditional approaches do not reflect the contemporary world and teaching approaches must reflect modern-day student needs (Price-Dennis, 2016). Mainstream education is failing to address the current realities and does not reflect the changes that have taken place in social spheres regarding racial oppression. There is still subtle oppression that remains in racialized institutions. Silence, along with the assumption that injury caused by this form of racism is negligible, is misplaced as evidence suggests that it has a long-term impact on the people of color (Ohito, 2018). Therefore, culturally responsive teaching not only benefits non-white students; it also benefits the white, middle-class students, and even English-speaking families, that make it a highly transformative strategy. When integrated into the classroom, the benefits of CRT revolve around strengthening each learner's sense of identity, increasing student engagement with the learning material, ensuring that equity and inclusivity exist in all learning contexts, and supporting creative and critical thinking.

8   Decolonization Curricula in Creating Equitable Opportunities

According to King (2014), the historical foundation of writing glorifies Western ethnocentrism, and it is this racial apparatus that has promoted the rift between white people and people of color. For instance, almost all PK–12 social studies books have been written by white educators and historians and have created perceptions of Black people as being second-class citizens. It was normal to view Black skin as a curse, and people with this skin were seen as barbarians with little humanity, lacking intelligence and in need of civilization. There have been movements initiated by African American educators that have focused on creating theoretical and practical multicultural and social studies resources to balance racism, but there is still much to be done. King (2014) suggests an alternative Black curricular framework to rewrite Blacks' history. This is because mainstream textbooks and other materials listed in the curriculum promote social and intellectual conformity and endorse citizenship that respects white supremacist tenets.

Decolonization is alive in many books, steered by academic performance, common sense, cultural patterns, peoples' self-images, personal aspirations, and many more modern education aspects. In considering these factors, measures must be undertaken to provide equal educational opportunities to all students (Nash, 2013). First, the decolonization of the mind involves eliminating taboos and norms that reinforce colonialism. This takes place in stages, as people relate with their past, present, and future.

Allen (2019) believes that issues and discussions about race are not to be avoided. Instead, racial literacy should be used to develop cultural competence among teachers and students. Since the main aim is to diversify the teaching workforce, culturally competent teachers are necessary. Suppose a teacher contextualizes his or her own racial identity within the legal frameworks of social institutions. In that case, he or she becomes better positioned to connect with students and guide them through the process of gaining cultural competency. The teacher can discuss identity issues encountered while schooling, among other racial issues that affect learners (Muhammad, 2020).

Internalized racism has affected many learners and teachers in equal measure. Experiences noted by Allen (2019) that were shared through a teacher identified as Marcus indicate how important cultural relevance and critical consciousness that is based on socio-historical knowledge is when it comes to people of color. To Marcus, curricular healing is fundamental, and it has to be intentional. The mainstream curriculum has historically marginalized certain students, and for these students to feel culturally affirmed or empowered, they need a curriculum that decentralizes whiteness. Deconstructing and reconstructing distorted information and curricular resources like textbooks is a step in creating and promoting equal educational opportunities and rebalancing historical information. For example, during lessons about international mining, learners should be informed of those lands' Indigenous occupants and the violence and exploitation they face (Mahiri, 2017). Social justice and self-discrimination are also enhanced through this process.

Decolonization helps people of color to identify their worth and eradicate the negative and inferior portrayals of them compared to Western cultures (Navarro, 2018). Advocates assert that the highly Westernized education system must be accommodative of diverse cultures, particularly the histories of people of color. Incorporating Black literature, for example, into the curriculum presents advantages because such knowledge fosters inclusion; it broadens all students' perspectives, including Black students' and those of their white peers.

One of the main objectives of schooling is to promote social cohesion, since education is established as the main revolutionary process for all societies. If education is inclusive, vulnerable groups are empowered. The curriculum significantly influences how young learners view knowledge, and it affects how they internalize knowledge construction. For instance, Charles (2019) argues that a lack of Black teachers symbolizes that teaching is a profession reserved for white teachers, and Black students will less likely select teaching as a profession. A deeper meaning is required when it comes to the understanding that controls education for US students. Since school is a fundamental aspect of society, as well as a functional culture, then school should reflect the diversity of this society. Culture is not simply observance of celebrations and rituals; instead, culture should be understood as the invisible meaning in which all societal entities' function. Nothing takes place outside of culture. A culture should furthermore provide solutions to problems. Where a culture fails to solve a problem, it should keep evolving to meet its members' needs. Stakeholders in education should have sufficient knowledge to comprehend the purpose of education, its cultural intent, and how the curriculum can solve the challenges faced by society. Curricula transmit certain principles, values, and interests, and untruths should be eliminated (hooks, 2000).

The underrepresentation of Black people and other minority groups is evident in US educational institutions. If they are the minority, then their voices can easily be silenced (Johnson, Boutte, Greene, & Smith, 2018). These students might have culturally specific ideas that they want to share and seek their inclusion in the curriculum. However, due to a lack of numbers and the democratic nature of systems where numbers are important, their ideas are dismissed. This does not mean that white educators cannot fight for decolonization. However, there is evidence point out that the colonized white spaces have oppressed people of color who exist in an environment that is dominated by Eurocentrism and whiteness. As such, efforts to separate issues of race from the issues of decolonization are very tedious. The issues of poor representation for people of color as well as whiteness and Eurocentric dominance directly indicate that the current hegemony needs to be rejected for decolonization to be successful. Already, oppression of people of color is highly normalized within the academy (Charles, 2019; Johnson et al., 2018).

Academicians from the marginalized races lack the opportunity to research and validate their work for inclusion in the curriculum. Even those who manage to get into their field and research, their findings to support the awareness of race inequality and curriculum decolonization become insignificant because they have few voices. However, it is apparent that the few available people of color offer their own view of institutional racism that is based on their lived experiences or what they observe from others. Such observations are not supposed to be marginalized; instead, they should be considered, shared, and applied in the decolonizing process. The white curriculum is based on the myth that if it is not white, then it is incorrect (Charles, 2019). Moreover, the exercise of people of color's traditions is limited since there is no chance to accommodate their perspectives and cultural values in the mainstream curriculum. Their practices are viewed as non-typical and below the academic standard. However, the marginalized therefore have opportunities to better their work in their disciplinary environments by being persistent, discussing their ideas in various forums and providing research points on curriculum decolonization (Hughes, 2011).

The main challenge in decolonizing the curriculum emanates from the fact that it is an issue affecting the majority. Consequently, the minority students of color are affected in regard to attainment. These are the individuals who require decolonization, and as such, decolonization is an issue for Black people. It is a challenging situation where people of color want to attain education equity amidst the underrepresentation, everyday racism, social agency, institutional racism, and the victim narrative. This means that the problems that are faced by the people of color in decolonizing institutions are complex and multifaceted and require more research (Singleton, 2015).

9   Culturally Relevant Pedagogy in Promoting Black Identity, Affirmation, and Resilience

A culturally responsive pedagogy incorporates attributes like classroom organization, instructional planning, cultural attributes, assessment, discipline, and motivational strategies. The learner's interest is cultivated by engaging their interest, inspiring achievement, and enhancing learning ownership in the whole process (Fasching-Varner & Dodo Seriki, 2012). The adoption of problem-based instruction, student involvement in projects, and active learning encourages learners' participation regardless of their cultural background. Black people in learning institutions have opportunities to boost their creativity based on their cultures (Nowakowski & Graves, 2017).

9.1   *Leading through Multicultural Identities*

Culturally relevant pedagogy entails experiencing leadership via racialized multicultural identities in which the participants rely on lived experiences in their communities, particularly their memories of operating in an environment that has culturally responsive care and support. There must likewise be a broad understanding of community that encompasses ethnic, professional, personal, organizational, and cultural communities (Muhammad & Haddix, 2016). Teachers must be equipped with skills that enable them to understand and communicate with Black students. To attain this, teachers who are from backgrounds that understand Black experiences should be incorporated into the system. These educators would work as school leaders and role models for

Black learners to ensure that racialized individuals feel that their identities are represented (Morris, 2019). Already, educators who have studied via institutions dominated by whiteness feel that they have a greater purpose to serve. These educators hone their leadership in a manner that they become a shining example of success for all students. Students who feel that an educator's leadership mirrors their lived experiences are more motivated and start to believe in the possibility of attaining their dreams (Love, 2019).

McArthur and Muhammad (2020) note that learners from marginalized communities should be encouraged to participate in courageous conversations and engage in dialogues about racialized oppression. Black communities require interventions to prepare them for leadership roles that confront racialized oppression, and this begins at the family level. This would facilitate a more systemic focus on equitable access to available resources and setting the curriculum in a way that caters to the needs of students who have challenges with second language acquisition and use. As such, an area of interest also includes classroom management to eliminate any bias held by teachers (McArthur & Muhammad, 2020). Irrespective of the shortcomings, the Black community must fight for leadership positions – one's disadvantages should be a motivation to seek more leadership opportunities because it is through such leadership that the system can be changed. Experiences in racial oppression should develop fortitude for Black leaders, and this would serve to increase voice and advocacy for increased representation of minorities.

The few Black leaders in education institutions require embracing fortitude in advocacy and activism for a system that values equity. Martinez, Armstrong, and Cerela (2017) suggest that these leaders can even infuse culturally responsive pedagogical teaching when preparing critical professional development opportunities. Some of these steps require sacrifice and courage because they do not currently exist in institutions dominated by whiteness. A leader taking such a step may opt not to seek permission because doing so would create unnecessary barriers – the system is not designed for that, and convincing many players when one is the minority is challenging (McArthur & Muhammad, 2020). Such depictions of courage emanate from different interactions in the community, and Black educators' must maintain fortitude in applying culturally relevant pedagogical practices in teaching to improve the learning experiences of the students.

The Black community must explicitly engage in knowledge creation and prejudice reduction. Such efforts cannot be initiated with the required seriousness by white people; such initiative requires beginning from those affected by oppressive racism (Lindsay-Dennis, 2015) and engaging aspiring educators from racialized communities in critical conversations that require these individuals to review how racial bias has shaped their interactions and how this might affect their relationships with learners. Doing so would help these individuals become pillars in transforming biases that would end up changing climates and cultures in their schools. Through Black learners and educators situating their work in the community, family, and the future of their children, they can develop leadership identities and skills that are situated in what King (2014) refers to as social justice orientation. Such leadership needs to be shaped by the Black community's lived experiences, and this will lead to multicultural identities in which the spirit of not giving up would be transferred to learners.

9.2 *Leadership Based on Multiconsciousness (Race, Resilience, and Resistance)*

When leaders in universities are equipped with skills for understanding the interlocking nature of the multilayered oppressions, they increase awareness of the nature of the war that is being fought. One is likely to experience racial battle fatigue when one realizes that the war is not likely to end any time soon (Acevedo, 2020). After so many experiences of racialized microaggressions, people of color may end up internalizing racism, and this triggers the unconscious acceptance of this hierarchy. People of color may be engulfed by despair and apathy as microaggressions continue to dominate despite their resistance. The battle becomes psychological, emotional, social, and spiritual at the same time. To avoid internalizing racism and to alleviate the injuries that result from this, individuals of color in education require self-work to avoid spiritual breakdown. Leaders require constant self-affirmation because racialized nihilism is systemic, institutionalized, accompanied by violence, and takes place daily (Lindsay-Dennis, 2015). One's internal sense of value and worth should be motivated by desire and concern for self in the community as well as that of others. Such a battle will always occur in the course of leadership for any person interested in changing the racialized education system. Without caution and being aware of the repercussions, leaders may experience stress and trauma resulting from failed expectations.

9.3 *Resilience and Resistance as Components of Leadership*

Those from minority communities face many challenges in institutional leadership roles. First, it is notable that these leaders may become stressed or traumatized when there is the need to implement policies and practices that go against their beliefs of social justice. If one fails to implement school reforms that are against their stand or policies and practices that are against their beliefs regarding cultural perspectives in the learning system, evaluations label them as failures. Further, there is also limited funding for programs that are managed by people of color. School disciplinary policies are also racialized to the extent that Black boys are afraid to volunteer or participate in leadership positions (Rothstein, 2015).

When in leadership, Black individuals experience psychological, emotional, physical, and spiritual reactions related to racialized stress and trauma that detracts from their focus on multicultural knowledge reforms and drains their intellectual capital. However, when these leaders revisit their lived experiences and what motivated them to get into leadership, they can renew the strength to reclaim their value and worth. The climate in which they operate might fail to acknowledge their existence, but resistance and resilience will bear fruits in the future (Allen, 2019).

Black leaders cultivate resilience from their multicultural lived experiences and continued experiences as leaders. Being an educational leader amid racialized (and perhaps gendered) oppression can reshape and resharpen one's multicultural sensitivities, and this creates stronger, culturally specific resilience. Even while Black leaders in institutions dominated by racial microaggressions may be made to look oppositional or are silenced by the majority, marginalized, and, in some cases, pushed out, communities must lend increased support for these resilient educational leaders since they are humans with emotions and can get hurt (Johnson & Bryan, 2016).

10 Recommendations and Best Practices for Integration of Culturally Relevant Pedagogy in Education Programs and PK–12 Classrooms

Traditional teaching strategies focus on teacher-student dynamics. In this case, the teacher is the expert and works to adhere to a set curriculum that is standardized, and there are certain standardized tests to indicate that the student has received the knowledge. As per Dillard (2012), this type of teaching is outdated, and more dynamic approaches to teaching need to be used. Classrooms are more diverse today, and therefore, the instruction has to be different, building on individuals and their cultural and lived experiences. The education system and the teaching strategies that are used must be justice-oriented and reflect the social context of the contemporary world. To address these issues, Johnson and Bryan (2016) start by noting that the majority of educators are not poorly aware of social and equity issues in the classroom and the general population. Equity-based education methodologies receive a lot of opposition due to the lack of critical theoretical framing when educating teachers. There is the need to understand the plight of Black students in education, and this starts with knowledge conceptualization and knowledge that is valued or ignored. Scholars focusing on teacher education programs must embrace efforts that build multifaceted Black male identities to offer educators programs that can uplift and solicit the perspectives of this marginalized group (Johnson & Bryan, 2016).

The first way to do this can be found inside the classroom. Students learn blackness as problematic and also a position of deficit. Some use the term *disadvantaged* in which they are understood as a class of people who have absorbed oppression. These notions are difficult to change, but students can learn that being Black is not a birth curse or disadvantage. Further, in the classroom, some learners may even fail to respond to discussions about racism when asked about their long-held assumptions (Cook, 2015). Some white teachers may also totally ignore topics about race. This silence may signify unwillingness to take a racial position, and according to Allen (2019), this silence means that they have stereotypical assumptions about Black students. These issues can be tackled through the curriculum because avoiding topics of the race indicates that these educators fail to acknowledge the presence of systemic racism. Through a curriculum that discusses the histories of the colonizer and colonized as interrelated aspects and then acknowledges that these issues largely remain unspoken and not taught, the history and heritage of the people of color can be better understood. The curriculum should focus on an anti-racist and decolonial pedagogy that challenges any form of educational exclusion. Such exclusionary practices reinforce and reproduce dominant knowledge and the status quo.

Ylimaki and Jacobson (2013) suggest that culturally responsive teaching starts with acknowledging that old approaches to teaching and curriculum content were not wrong, but the focus should be on increasingly incorporating literature from other cultures. The curriculum should be restructured in a manner that accommodates the diverse array of authors and community workers today. Further, there should be a focus on finding the "hook and anchor" that may help attract learners to the syllabus content through the use of their experiences. In such a manner, these learners perceive themselves in relation to the perspectives of what they are reading and not just from the angle of the white, Western world. Learning becomes more experiential and enjoyable for students of color with content that reflects more of their heritage or culture.

By leveraging students' cultural backgrounds, an educator succeeds in activating their prior knowledge. Unlike before, contemporary teaching does not assume that students are blank slates. Instead, it acknowledges that students know something from their parents or community or the general social milieu. The assumption that the students enter the learning environment with diverse experiences is what Johnson et al. (2018) refer to as cultural capital.

To successfully engage these students in learning, the educator has to encourage the learners to draw on this prior knowledge to contribute to class discussions. Prior knowledge plays a highly pivotal role in their learning. Instead of focusing on whiteness to understand the literature, the students take a broader perspective.

To decolonize the curriculum, it has been highlighted that the curriculum has to reflect the learner's social community and not try to fit students of color into a curriculum that is dominated by whiteness. Such a move entails contextualizing the students' learning and increasing its relevance. If it is a history lesson, the educator must focus on explaining to the learner why this lesson or content are relevant to issues in the world today, either in the school or the community in general. The learning has to shift in a manner that encourages students to critically analyze their world (Muhammad, 2020).

A teacher needs to be a motivator who utilizes available resources to encourage learners to leverage their own cultural capital. All students do not come from the same background. Educators have a key role to play in ensuring that they do not offer an education that forces some students to rely on the cultural capital of others (Muhammad, 2020). This type of teaching derails the educational process for these students because the foreignness of others' cultures acts as a disadvantage to them. However, if a teacher encourages each student to analyze issues in reference to their own culture, these learners are empowered to use their cultural capital to increase their voice.

Another critical aspect that is overlooked in most cases is the classroom setup. It is difficult to attain all the changes at once, but slow advances towards more representational content can be transformative. A teacher can take an inventory of the books found in the library and ensure that what students read as the course material is composed of authors of diverse racial identities (Jordan, 2016). All minority cultures require to be considered, and authors of these resources must use culturally sensitive language and write about all types of families. All aspects of culture should be checked thoroughly before these resources are approved as class reading materials. These changes may seem small, but they make a huge difference when it comes to having a more culturally responsive classroom.

Another paramount move entails building relationships. Some students may be uncomfortable when dealing with some teachers and opt to avoid them in learning (Johnson et al., 2018). To remedy such cases, teachers have a responsibility to build relationships with students and try to understand their cultural background so that each student feels respected and valued. These relationships create new communities for these learners, and they develop a sense of belonging.

11   Conclusion

Educators can incorporate culturally responsive strategies to impact learners' lives. This entails using thoughtful and inclusive instruction to positively influence students, including employing culturally relevant pedagogy to affirm and promote Black identity and resilience by ensuring that all curriculum materials respectfully reflect Black culture. Schools require to be treated as spaces in which people are institutionalized to accept their position in society, and education should thus be acknowledged as a process that can be used to transform this society. Educators should always seek feedback from Black students on how they feel about the learning process and their understanding of the same. By doing this, Black students will be encouraged to participate more in the learning process and openly share their experiences.

White teachers should work to understand the meaning and impacts of racism by attending workshops as well as finding out how they can prevent racism in their everyday spaces and communities. Keeping quiet and avoiding race-related topics is equivalent to denying the presence of systemic racism. Teachers must proceed to educate their learners about the presence of systemic racism and look for solutions on how to eliminate it in their classrooms. Implementing culturally relevant pedagogy that meets all learners' needs is not easy for curriculum planners and educators. The success or failure of combining any culturally relevant pedagogy depends on the teacher, who possesses significant freedom to decide on the type of CRT to be used in various learning contexts. All students should be comfortable in the classroom, and a well-trained teacher should consider learners' social needs in addition to academic needs. Proper training should be conducted with future teachers as well as those currently practicing to equip them with knowledge about the implementation of culturally relevant pedagogy. Educators should have good relationships with each student, the student's family, and the entire community. This will lead to academic improvement because learners will see that they have individuals who care about their academic achievement and understand their familial and cultural context. They will then feel that they belong at the school and that the school is connected to their family.

References

Acevedo, M. C. (2020). *Bringing language to consciousness: Teacher professional learning in genre-based reading pedagogy* [Doctoral dissertation]. Open University.

Allen, K. M. (2019). Transformative vision: Unpacking the racial literacy practices of a Black male teacher with his Black male students. *Journal for Multicultural Education, 13*(1), 82–93. doi:10.1108/jme-04-2017-0029

Baker-Bell, A. (2020). *Linguistic justice: Black language, literacy, identity, and pedagogy.* Routledge.

Behizadeh, N. (2014). Xavier's take on authentic writing. *Journal of Adolescent & Adult Literacy, 58*(4), 289–298.

Bowman, B. T., Comer, J. P., & Johns, D. J. (2018). Addressing the African American achievement gap: Three leading educators issue a call to action. *YC Young Children, 73*(2), 14–23.

Cahalan, M., Perna, L. W., Yamashita, M., Wright, J., & Santillan, S. (2018). *Indicators of higher education equity in the United States: 2018 historical trend report.* Pell Institute for the Study of Opportunity in Higher Education.

Charles, M. (2019). Effective teaching and learning: Decolonizing the curriculum. *Journal of Black Studies, 50*(8), 731–766.

Cook, L. (2015). *US education: Still separate and unequal.* US News and World Report.

Dillard, C. B. (2012). *Learning to (re)member the things we've learned to forget: Endarkened feminisms, spirituality, & the sacred nature of research & teaching.* Peter Lang.

Fasching-Varner, K. J., & Dodo Seriki, V. (2012). Moving beyond seeing with our eyes wide shut. A response to "There is no culturally responsive teaching spoken here." *Democracy and Education, 20*(1), 5.

hooks, b. (2000). *All about love: New visions.* William Morrow (HarperCollins).

Howard, T. C., & Rodriguez-Scheel, A. (2017). Culturally relevant pedagogy 20 years later: Progress or pontificating? What have we learned, and where do we go? *Teachers College Record, 119*(1).

Hughes, S. (2011). Justice for all or justice for just us? Toward a critical race pedagogy of hope through Brown in urban education. *Urban Education, 46*(1), 99–110.

Johnson, L. L., Boutte, G., Greene, G., & Smith, D. E. (2018). *African diaspora literacy: The heart of transformation in K–12 schools and teacher education.* Lexington Books.

Johnson, L., & Bryan, N. (2016). Using our voices, losing our bodies: Michael Brown, Trayvon Martin, and the spirit murders of Black male professors in the academy. *Race Ethnicity, and Education, 20*(2), 163–177.

Johnson, L. L., Bryan, N., & Boutte, G. (2018). Show us the love: Revolutionary teaching in (un)critical times. *The Urban Review, 51*(1), 46–64. doi:10.1007/s11256-018-0488-3

Jordan, J. (2016). Jim Crow: The sequel. In D. Bay (Ed.), *Know thyself: An African-American poetic journey* (p. 107). On Point.

King, L. (2014). When lions write history: Black history textbooks, African American educators, and the alternative Black curriculum in social studies education. *Multicultural Education, 22*(1), 2–11.

Li, I. W., & Carroll, D. (2017). *Factors influencing university student satisfaction, dropout, and academic performance: An Australian higher education equity perspective.* National Centre for Student Equity in Higher Education, Curtin University.

Lindsay-Dennis, L. (2015). Black feminist-womanist research paradigm. *Journal of Black Studies, 46*(5), 506–520.

Love, B. (2019). *We want to do more than survive: Abolitionist teaching and the pursuit of educational freedom.* Beacon Press.

Mahiri, J. (2017). *Deconstructing race: Multicultural education beyond the color-blind.* Teachers College Press.

Martinez, V., Armstrong, A., & Cerela, B. (2017). Writing the experiences and (corporeal) knowledges of women of color into educational studies: A colloquium. *Pedagogy & (Im)Possibilities across Education Research (PIPER), 1*(1), 1–14.

McArthur, S. A., & Muhammad, G. E. (2020). Pens down, don't shoot: An analysis of how Black young women use language to fight back. *Urban Education*, 1–28. doi:10.1177/0042085919893734

Meatto, K. (2019). Still separate, still unequal: Teaching about school segregation and educational inequality. *New York Times*, p. 2.

Milner IV, H. R. (2017). Where's the race in culturally relevant pedagogy? *Teachers College Record, 119*(1).

Morris, M. W. (2019). *Sing a rhythm, dance a blues: Education for the liberation of Black and Brown girls.* The New Press.

Muhammad, G. (2020). *Cultivating genius: An equity framework for culturally and historically responsive literacy.* Scholastic.

Muhammad, G. E., & Haddix, M. (2016). Centering Black girls' ways of knowing: A historical review of literature on the multiple literacies of Black girls. *English Education, 48*(4), 299–336.

Nash, J. C. (2013). Practicing love: Black feminism, love-politics, and post-intersectionality. *Meridians, 11*(2), 1–24.

Navarro, O. (2018). We can't do this alone: Validating and inspiring social justice teaching through a community of transformative praxis. *Curriculum Inquiry, 48*(3), 335–358.

Nowakowski, A. C., & Graves, K. Y. (2017). Does inflammation mediate relationships between racial identity and the onset of menopause among US adults? *Journal of Racial and Ethnic Health Disparities, 4*(6), 1128–1137.

Ohito, E. O. (2018). "I just love Black people!": Love, pleasure, and critical pedagogy in urban teacher education. *The Urban Review, 51*(1), 123–145.

Peterson, E. R., Rubie-Davies, C., Osborne, D., & Sibley, C. (2016). Teachers' explicit expectations and implicit prejudiced attitudes to educational achievement: Relations with student achievement and the ethnic achievement gap. *Learning and Instruction, 42*, 123–140.

Price-Dennis, D. (2016). Developing curriculum to support Black girls' literacies in digital spaces. *English Education, 48*(4), 337–361.

Rothstein, R. (2015). The racial achievement gap, segregated schools, and segregated neighborhoods: A constitutional insult. *Race and social problems, 7*(1), 21–30.

Saavedra, C. M., & Pérez, M. S. (2012). Chicana and Black feminisms: Testimonios of theory, identity, and multiculturalism. *Equity & Excellence in Education, 45*(3), 430–443. doi:10.1080/10665684.2012.681970

Sian, K. P. (2019). *Navigating institutional racism in British universities.* Springer International Publishing.

Singleton, G. E. (2015). *Courageous conversations about race: A field guide for achieving equity in schools.* Sage.

Webb, M., & Thomas, R. (2015). Teachers' perceptions of educators' and students' role in closing the achievement gap. *National Forum of Teacher Education Journal, 25*(3).

Ylimaki, R., & Jacobson, S. (2013). School leadership practice and preparation: Comparative perspectives on organizational learning (OL), instructional leadership (IL), and culturally responsive practices (CRP). *Journal of Educational Administration, 51*(1), 6–23.

CHAPTER 6

HBCUs as a Pathway to Becoming a Scientist

Institutional Characteristics of HBCUs That Are among the Top Baccalaureate Origins of Black Doctorate Recipients in STEM

Ivory A. Toldson, Mercy Mugo, Jennifer Hudson, Mahlet Megra and Cynthia Overton

Historically Black colleges and universities (HBCUs) offer African American high school graduates the best opportunity to eventually receive a doctorate in a science, technology, engineering, and mathematics (STEM) discipline. According to the National Science Foundation (NSF),[1] nearly 30% of Black science and engineering (S&E) doctorate recipients earned their bachelor's degree from HBCUs. However, HBCUs represent less than 3% of all institutions of higher education. This research explores common institutional characteristics among HBCUs that rank among the highest nationally for graduating undergraduate students who eventually earn an S&E doctorate. In addition, the study identifies HBCUs that do not rank among the highest nationally but have institutional characteristics that are similar to top-ranking HBCUs. We performed exploratory qualitative and quantitative analyses of archival data from three US Department of Education sources. The findings can advance our understanding of what works at HBCUs to enable undergraduate students to subsequently obtain (S&E) doctorates, which can have broader implications for diversifying the future STEM workforce.

1 Introduction and Context

The current composition of the science, technology, engineering, and mathematics (STEM) workforce does not reflect the racial diversity of the United States (Government Accountability Office, 2018). College educated African Americans[2] make up 7% of the STEM workforce (Graf, Fry, & Funk, 2018) but 13% of the US population (United States Census Bureau, 2018). Of the total science and engineering (S&E) degrees awarded in 2016, only 9% of those were awarded to African American students (National Science Foundation, 2019).

STEM and S&E, represented similarly in the research, describe a set of college majors, occupations and learning contexts that promote scientific, computational, and technological advancements (Toldson, 2018). Creating conditions that foster the success of Black students in college can increase Black representation in STEM and S&E disciplines. Although HBCUs represent 3% of the nation's institutions of higher learning, and despite low endowment and modest resources, they have made substantial contributions to the number of STEM degrees earned by African Americans (Strayhorn, Williams, Tillman-Kelly, & Suddeth, 2012).

In 2012, HBCUs awarded 16% of bachelor's degrees, 11% of master's degrees, and 12% of doctoral degrees in science and engineering to Black or African Americans (NSF, 2015). HBCUs also consistently rank among the nation's top baccalaureate-origin institutions for a significant proportion of Black S&E doctoral recipients.

Research is needed to determine the common characteristics of HBCUs that graduate Black STEM students to develop models for other HBCUs and non-HBCUs that replicate their success. Developing such models is a national imperative, because the United States will need one million more STEM professionals in the next decade than institutions are currently slated to produce (US Bureau of Labor Statistics, 2015). This research explores the institutional characteristics of HBCUs that are among the top baccalaureate origins of Black doctorate recipients in science and engineering, and these findings have broader implications for diversifying the STEM workforce.

2 Literature Review

According to a 2016 report from the US Department of Education, HBCUs comprise twenty-one of the top fifty institutions producing Black graduates who eventually earn their doctorates in S&E (US Department of Education, 2016). The literature reviewed in this section explores possible reasons why a disproportionately high number of Black students who earn doctorates in S&E received their undergraduate degrees at HBCUs. The review includes two sections: (1) STEM degree production at HBCUs; and (2) research on institutional characteristics and HBCU STEM production.

2.1 *STEM Degree Production at HBCUs*

HBCUs share a common mission: to provide and increase educational opportunities for underserved communities. HBCUs are uniquely positioned to increase the pipeline of Black students who go on to pursue advanced degrees and careers in STEM. While describing the influential role of HBCUs in educating future STEM professionals, a report by the NSF stated that "HBCUs have an outsized impact on preparing students for S&E doctoral programs" (NSF,

2019, p. 8). Although HBCUs represent 3% of the nation's institutions of higher learning, they remain among the nation's top baccalaureate-origin institutions for African American S&E doctoral recipients (Toldson, 2019). In order of ranking, NSF's top-fifty list for institutions graduating Black students that earn S&E doctorates includes twenty-one HBCUs: Howard University, Spelman College, Florida A&M University, Hampton University, Xavier University of Louisiana, Morehouse College, Morgan State University, North Carolina A&T State University, Southern University and A&M College, Tuskegee University, Jackson State University, Tennessee State University, Alabama A&M University, Clark Atlanta University, Prairie View A&M University, Tougaloo College, Norfolk State University, North Carolina Central University, Grambling State University, Dillard University, and Fisk University (US Department of Education, 2016). The twenty-one institutions represent ten states and the District of Columbia.

Interestingly, the non-HBCUs on the NSF's top-fifty list differ greatly from HBCUs. According to the Carnegie Classification of Institutions of Higher Education (2020), among the twenty-nine predominantly white Institutions (PWIs), all but four have a Carnegie classification of "Very High Research Activity" or "Research One" (R1). Among the twenty-one HBCUs, none have a Carnegie classification of "Very High Research Activity" and only two have a classification of "High." Yet none of the PWIs, such as Georgia State University (Black enrollment = 14,039), Troy University (Black enrollment = 8,694), and University of Memphis (Black enrollment = 8,337), which possess an enrollment of Black students that is larger than most single HBCUs, made NSF's list of the top fifty institutions. Per the Integrated Postsecondary Education Data System (IPEDS) (2020), 137 nonprofit four-year PWIs had a Black enrollment that was greater than the HBCU average Black enrollment of 2,629; however, only four of them are on the top-fifty list. In total, among the top fifty institutions, HBCUs collectively produced 1,819 Black graduates who earned a doctorate in S&E, while PWIs produced 1,600 Black graduates, and foreign institutions produced 798 Black graduates.

HBCUs continue to make strides in helping advance the representation of minorities in STEM/S&E fields (NSF, 2019). Although HBCUs represent a small proportion of all institutions in the United States, they were responsible for awarding bachelor's degrees to 15% of Black or African Americans in 2016 and they were the primary undergraduate home for 25% of graduates who earned S&E doctorates between 2013 and 2017 (NSF, 2019).

2.2 Research on Institutional Characteristics and HBCU STEM Production

Toldson and Esters (2012) used the Minority Male STEM Initiative (MMSI Campus Survey) to develop a theory of change to understand factors associated with HBCUs' success in graduating students in STEM. The purpose of the MMSI Campus Survey was to understand how university administrators, STEM faculty, and students of color in STEM disciplines navigate the path to recruiting, retaining, and graduating underrepresented students in STEM disciplines. The MMSI Campus Survey study focused on 1,442 underrepresented STEM students across fourteen institutions, including three HBCUs.

Factor analysis of the survey responses revealed three factors: (1) faculty relationships, (2) belonging, and (3) academic pressure. Using regression estimates, a factor score was assigned to each participant; these were used to compare means across institution types. Results indicated that students at HBCUs were significantly more likely than students at PWIs to have better relationships with faculty and to feel a higher sense of "belonging."

Other studies on HBCUs' production of STEM graduates reveal a myriad of factors that provide a theoretical basis for exploring the institutional and student characteristics that may explain the variance between HBCUs that are successful with graduating STEM students who eventually obtain doctorates and those that are less successful. Specific findings include the following points:

HBCUs have a unique structure that could foster a more supportive environment for STEM students. Studies indicate that the mentoring that occurs naturally from HBCU faculty having higher teaching loads and more contact with undergraduate students can produce positive outcomes for HBCU STEM students (Kendricks, Nedunuri, & Arment, 2013). The number of faculty members of color at HBCUs, specifically Black faculty members (Jett, 2013) that understood Black culture (Gasman & Nguyen, 2016; Toldson, 2013), was cited as a factor that enhanced mentoring and student success at HBCUs in the existing literature.

HBCUs have developed policies and practices to accommodate and advance STEM students with less academic preparation and fewer resources. HBCUs serve students from low socioeconomic backgrounds, first-generation college students, and students who are academically underprepared for college education. When such student characteristics are controlled, research suggest that HBCUs outperform many of their peer institutions in retaining and graduating students (Richards & Awokoya, 2012). HBCUs educate a cross-section of STEM students, including first-generation college students and community college transfers (Jackson, 2013; Smith, 2016). Through a meta-synthesis, one study investigated HBCUs' role in preparing first-generation STEM students and found several unique aspects of HBCU STEM learning environments: assessing prior academic performance; facilitating college adjustment; social integration; and academic socialization (Hicks & Wood, 2016).

Another study demonstrated how some HBCUs use "retention theories" to keep lesser prepared STEM students through interviews with STEM program coordinators at HBCUs (Palmer, Davis, & Thompson, 2010). Another study also found that HBCUs provide early supports for underrepresented STEM students to help mitigate the challenges presented by mathematics as an access point for STEM entry (Adams, Robinson, Covington, & Talley-Matthews, 2017), including through summer bridge programs (Fakayode, Yakubu, Adeyeye, Pollard, & Mohammed, 2014). These supports have shown to effectively facilitate the progress of HBCU STEM students.

HBCUs' use of culturally relevant pedagogical approaches foster the academic success of STEM students. Several research studies postulate that HBCUs advance STEM education among African American students because of the connection between racial identity development (Brown, Mangram, Sun, Cross, & Raab, 2017), critical race theory (Adams et al., 2017; Lundy-Wagner, 2013) and Black student achievement. These studies reinforce the impact of shared cultural experiences, understanding the role of racism and discrimination on opportunities, and the socio-cognitive benefits of being exposed to highly educated Black people. Intersectional issues associated with Black women and Black men in STEM at HBCUs have also been observed (Perna et al., 2009).

2.3 Gaps in the Literature

The literature highlights many unifying features that appear to be related to HBCUs successfully preparing and graduating underrepresented minority students in STEM. However, there are many unanswered questions. For instance, many of these studies observed the normal practices and policies of HBCUs without clearly indicating if the practices occur naturally because of African American cultural nuances or strategically to accommodate their students. In addition, analyses of institutional and student characteristics reveal vast diversity among HBCUs' institutional characteristics (Simms & Bock, 2014). It is not completely clear whether variation in the success of HBCUs is a function of lack of knowledge transfer between institutions or because of resource differences between the higher-performing HBCUs and HBCUs with lower performance levels. More research is necessary to help us to distill the unique student and institutional characteristics that are associated with HBCUs successfully preparing and graduating STEM students.

3 Theoretical Framework

This study is grounded in institutional theory, a sociological framework that explains the influence that institutional conformity to symbolic actions has on the formal structures of organizations (Meyer & Rowan, 1977; Tolbert &

Zucker, 1996). DiMaggio and Powell's (1983) foundational research describes how the institutional environment pressures organizations to be *isomorphic*, or similar to each other, in form and practice. This occurs through three processes: (1) *coercive isomorphism*, in which formal or informal forces are applied on the organization by the government, other organizations, or the cultural expectations of the environment in which they are embedded; (2) *mimetic isomorphism* or the uncertainty in goals, technology, or market trends that lead organizational decision makers to adopt structures and practices that replicate other exemplary organizations in their fields; and, (3) *normative isomorphism*, encompassing principles and cognitive frameworks that are developed and controlled by standards-making bodies (DiMaggio & Powell, 1983). Institutional change results as powerful actors within institutionalized fields make decisions that tend to make their organizations more alike.

Generally, institutions of higher education have a common organizational structure – yet institutional theory offers a lens by which to better understand the ways in which HBCUs may have unique structures and isomorphic influences. Theoretically, HBCUs have formal organizational structures with symbolic aspects. The symbolic aspects (e.g., mission and executive leadership) influence HBCUs' structures and practices and are motivated by the need for legitimacy and survival. Understanding formal HBCU structures from this perspective enabled our research team to explore the underlying, complex network that contributes to HBCUs producing more Black undergraduates who eventually become scientists than most other institutions of higher education.

Although institutional theories have not been developed to their full potential as they primarily include a preponderance of Eurocentric orientations and lack adaptation to the HBCU experience, the theory of change for this study considers deep issues of symbolism, traditions, and macro-level isomorphic influences that are unique to HBCUs. In many ways, the HBCU experience mirrors the Black experience. Noted scholar W. E. B. Du Bois opined about the duality of Black existence, as we try to affirm our culture while conforming to mainstream standards, often as a strategy for survival.

Therefore, the institutional factors that we use for this study – that is, (1) admissions, size, and growth; (2) graduation, retention, and financial aid; (3) fiscal resources and assets; and (4) capacity, administration tenure, and faculty resources – which were largely derived from mainstream academic standards, must be viewed within the proper cultural contexts. Institutional theory helps us to conceptualize the dilemma of the modern HBCU, which, through normative and coercive isomorphism, has to adhere to the same standards as PWIs while striving to serve a student population with needs that may be incompatible with these standards. Specifically, we seek to investigate the institutionalized context of HBCUs' policies and programs, which can serve as

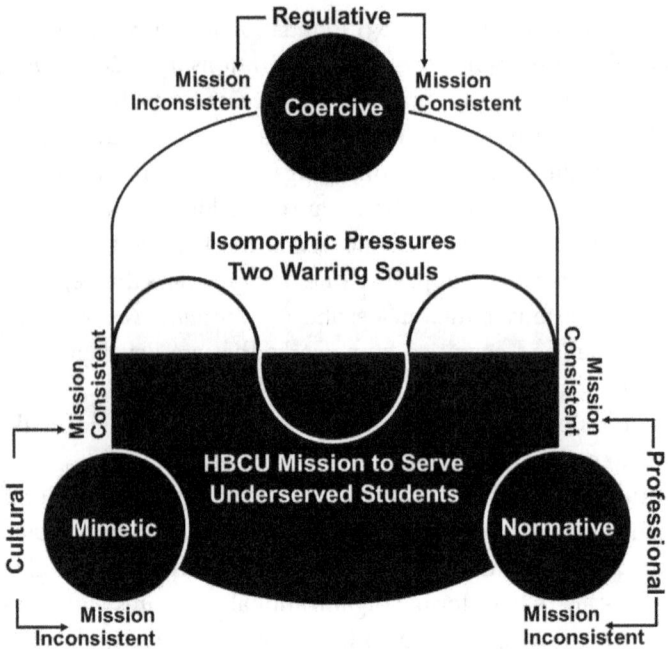

FIGURE 6.1 A Du Boisian adaptation of the three isomorphic pressures (DiMaggio & Powell, 1983) that influence institutional policies and practices at HBCUs in ways that can be inconsistent with their mission to serve underserved students

powerful traditions that influence students' motivation and desire to achieve. This research will allow us to contribute new insights on institutional theory as it applies to institutions of higher education.

3.1 Purpose

This study seeks to answer a simple yet very important question: How do HBCUs, which generally have smaller enrollments and fewer resources, achieve success in graduating Black students who earn doctorates in S&E at a pace only observed among the nation's R1 institutions? Obvious institutional characteristics, such as size and research designation, do not distinguish HBCUs that appear on the NSF list from HBCUs and PWIs that did not. Therefore, this study is necessary for national efforts to reveal the unique factors associated with diversifying the S&E workforce that have only been observed in HBCUs of diverse Carnegie classifications and a uniform group PWIs comprised mostly of R1 institutions.

3.2 Research Questions

Research Question 1: What are the common institutional demographic variables among the twenty-one HBCUs that rank in the top fifty for producing

Black baccalaureate graduates who go on to earn doctorates in STEM and are any of the institutions "outliers?"

Research Question 2: What are the "emerging" HBCUs, defined as HBCUs that do not rank in the top fifty for producing Black baccalaureate graduates who go on to earn doctorates in STEM, but have institutional characteristics that are most similar to "anchor" HBCUs, which do rank in the top fifty?

4   Method

Of the one hundred recognized HBCUs in the United States, community colleges, medical colleges, and one institution that closed in the spring of 2018 were excluded from the study, leaving a total of eighty-six HBCUs. These eighty-six HBCUs include the twenty-one HBCUs on the NSF's top-fifty list, which we refer to as anchor institutions. We refer to the remaining sixty-five HBCUs in the study as non-anchor institutions. The sample represents diverse institutions of higher education; 43% are public, 65% are located in cities; and the average enrollment across these institutions is 2,997. Table 6.1 displays the general characteristics of HBCUs that were selected for the study.

As mentioned above, this study used archival data from publicly available sources. Variables were selected from three US Department of Education data sources: the Integrated Postsecondary Education Data System (IPEDS),[3] the Database of Accredited Postsecondary Institutions and Programs (DAPIP), and the Federal Student Aid (FSA) Data Center. A large range of measures are available for use to better understand institutions of higher education. For example, IPEDS alone, as the core federal source for higher education information, has 250 variables.

First, we used past research (Toldson & Esters, 2012) to develop a list of potential variables. Next, we consulted experts in higher education research

TABLE 6.1   Basic characteristics of institutions

	Overall	Anchor institutions	Non-anchor institutions
Total number	86	21	65
Percent public	43%	52%	42%
Percent in city	65%	85%	58%
Average enrollment	2,997	5,084	2,312

Note: Rounded to the nearest whole number.

to narrow the list. As a result, twenty-eight substantial variables were selected for this study (see Table 6.2). Twenty-five variables were retrieved or derived[4] from the IPEDS dataset. Accreditation data was retrieved from the DAPIP and cohort default rate was retrieved from the FSA Data Center. Variables were grouped into five topical categories (see Table 6.2). To categorize these variables, we first performed exploratory factor analysis to assess whether there are discreet constructs that provide similar information. The results from

TABLE 6.2   Categories and source variables used to characterize institutions

Financial resources	Revenue
	Grants and contracts
	Appropriations
	Endowment
Academic and research expenditures	Instruction expenses as percentage of core expenses
	Research expenses as percentage of core expenses
	Academic support expenses as percentage of core expenses
	Instructional support expenses as percentage of core expenses
	Student services expenses as percentage of core expenses
	Average faculty salary
Institutional environment	Carnegie size and setting
	Accreditation status
	Proportion of STEM degrees conferred
	Degree of urbanization
	Student-to-faculty ratio
Faculty profile	Percent of faculty members with tenure
	Percent of faculty members who are African American
Student profile and outcomes	12-month enrollment
	12-month enrollment stability
	Male-to-female ratio
	ACT composite 75th percentile score
	Selectivity
	Admissions yield
	Percentage Pell eligible
	Percentage awarded federal student loans
	Retention rate
	Graduation rate
	Cohort default rate

the factor analysis, while suggesting some groupings, did not result in identification of factors whereby the variables were strongly related to that factor (nearly all variables had factor loadings below 0.75). Moreover, the variables that were grouped under one factor did not always show clear theoretical patterns. Hence, we supplemented these results with a qualitative evaluation and categorized the variables into metrics that inform the *financial measures, academic and research expenditure, institutional environment, faculty profile*, and *student profile and outcomes*. The definition of each of the variables used is available in Table 6.2.

4.1 Data Analysis

To address research question 1 and identify the common institutional demographic variables among these twenty-one HBCUs, referred to hereafter as anchor institutions, we assessed institutional administrative data among anchor institutions and compared to other HBCUs. Data analysis was carried out using Stata (version 15) software. After cleaning the data, frequencies and summary statistics were generated (see Table 6.3).

To address research question 2 and determine what an emerging institution is and identify emerging institutions among HBCUs included in the study, the research team devised a scoring system based on the average and standard deviation of all anchor institutions for all the variables shown in Table 6.2.[5] Each of the eighty-six institutions in the analysis received a score of either 0, 1, or 2 for each of the twenty-five variables based on how similar they are to an average anchor institution. For instance, if the average enrollment size for all anchor institutions is 5,000 and the standard deviation is 2,000, institutions that are one (or more) standard deviation below the average received a score of 0. Institutions that are within one standard deviation of the average received a score of 1 and institutions that are one (or more) standard deviation above the average received a score of 2.[6]

Measures for which a low score might inaccurately indicate better performance were "back coded." These measures were selectivity (percentage admitted), percentage Pell grant awarded, percentage awarded federal student loans, cohort default rate, and student-to-faculty ratio. Then the amounts of 0s, 1s, and 2s were tallied for each institution to determine each institution's proximity to an average anchor institution. The score for non-anchor institutions ranged from 8 (Harris-Stowe State University) to 30 (Bowie State University). The score for anchor institutions ranged from 18 (Alabama A&M University) to 35 (Howard University). Lastly, the average score between all institutions with a score that matches the anchors (between 18 and 35) was used to identify the

TABLE 6.3 Summary statistics of assessed continuous variables for analysis

Variable	All institutions				Anchor institutions				Non-anchor institutions			
	Sample size	Average	Median	Standard deviation	Sample size	Average	Median	Standard deviation	Sample size	Average	Median	Standard deviation
Financial resources												
Revenue (in millions)	86	$89	$55	$113	21	$194	$160	$180	65	$56	$38	$51
Grants and contracts (in millions)	86	$21	$14	$20	21	$40	$42	$19	65	$15	$9	$17
Appropriations (in millions)	86	$20	$5	$32	21	$44	$27	$55	65	$13	$3	$19
Endowment (in millions)	86	$38	$11	$79	21	$106	56	$141	65	$18	$9	$28
Academic expenditures												
Instruction expenses as percentage of core expenses	86	32	31	10	21	34	34	7	65	32	30	11
Research expenses as percentage of core expenses	86	5	2	6	21	9	9	4	65	3	0	6
Academic support expenses as percentage of core expenses	86	10	9	5	21	11	12	4	65	9	8	5
Instructional support expenses as percentage of core expenses	86	27	26	12	21	22	20	8	65	29	29	13

(cont.)

TABLE 6.3 Summary statistics of assessed continuous variables for analysis (cont.)

Variable	All institutions				Anchor institutions				Non-anchor institutions			
	Sample size	Average	Median	Standard deviation	Sample size	Average	Median	Standard deviation	Sample size	Average	Median	Standard deviation
Student services expenses as percentage of core expenses	86	13	12	7	21	10	10	5	65	14	13	7
Average faculty salary (in thousands)	86	$56	$54	$14	21	$64	$65	$11	65	$53	$51	$14
Institutional environment												
Proportion of STEM degrees conferred	79	0.2	0.2	0.1	21	0.2	0.2	0.1	58	0.1	0.1	0.1
Student-to-faculty ratio	85	15	15	4	21	15	15	4	64	15	15	3
Faculty profile												
Percent of faculty members with tenure	71	42	47	17	21	47	49	12	50	40	41	18
Percent of faculty members who are African American	86	60	62	17	21	60	62	11	65	60	62	18

(cont.)

TABLE 6.3 Summary statistics of assessed continuous variables for analysis (cont.)

Variable	All institutions				Anchor institutions				Non-anchor institutions			
	Sample size	Average	Median	Standard deviation	Sample size	Average	Median	Standard deviation	Sample size	Average	Median	Standard deviation
Student profile and student outcomes												
Enrollment	85	2997	2166	2504	21	5084	5405	2915	64	2312	1694	1933
10-year enrollment percent change	84	7	−6	63	21	−6	−6	15	63	11	−5	72
Male-to-female ratio	84	.8	.7	.4	20	.6	.5	.2	64	.8	.7	.4
ACT composite 75th percentile score	57	20	20	3	20	22	22	3	37	19	19	2
Selectivity	62	57	51	21	20	61	63	20	42	55	49	22
Admissions yield	62	23	20	12	20	24	21	10	42	22	20	12
Percent Pell awarded	85	69	71	15	21	60	62	14	64	71	73	14
Percent awarded Federal student loans	85	75	77	16	21	74	75	9	64	75	78	17
Retention rate	84	63	63	12	21	73	72	9	63	60	60	11
Graduation rate	84	32	31	15	21	41	39	12	63	29	25	15
Cohort default rate	85	17	15	7	21	12	12	4	64	18	18	7

emerging institutions. This average score was a tallied value of 23 and was used as a cutoff value of determining the emerging institutions.

5 Results

5.1 *Research Question 1*

Research question 1 asks: What are the common institutional demographic variables among the twenty-one HBCUs that rank in the top fifty for producing Black baccalaureate graduates who go on to earn doctorates in STEM and are any of the institutions "outliers?"

To determine this, frequencies and summary statistics were run on twenty-eight variables that were grouped into the five topical categories indicated above across all HBCUs, across the anchor institutions, and across the non-anchor institutions. Results are presented in Table 6.3 for the continuous variables and in Table 6.4 for the categorical variables. The unweighted sample mean values primarily indicated differences across anchor and non-anchor institutions. While the mean values tended to show substantial differences between anchor and non-anchor institutions, in some cases there were commonalities.

5.1.1 Financial Resources

An institution's financial resources are defined by its yearly revenue and endowment. While non-anchor institutions had a median yearly revenue of approximately $36 million in 2016–17, anchor institutions had more than four times the revenue, with a median of $160 million in the same year. Consistent with this ratio, non-anchor institutions had $9.0 million of revenue from grants and contracts, while anchor institutions had $42 million. In addition to yearly revenue, institutions can also draw from their endowment, and anchor institutions have the advantage here as well. For non-anchor institutions, more than 70% of them had an endowment that was less than $25 million, whereas only about 25% of anchor institutions had less than this amount. Moreover, more than half of the anchor institutions had a larger endowment than almost all the non-anchor institutions.[7]

5.1.2 Academic and Research Expenditures

At anchor institutions, average faculty salaries are higher by 20% when looking at salaries for instructional staff at all ranks. Moreover, anchor institutions foster a research environment more so than non-anchor institutions. For thirty-four of the sixty-five (52%) non-anchor institutions, expenditure on research made up 0% of their core expenses, whereas this was true for only one of the

TABLE 6.4 Summary statistics of assessed categorical variables for analysis

Variable	All institutions		Anchor institutions		Non-anchor institutions	
	Number	Percent	Number	Percent	Number	Percent
Institutional environment						
Carnegie size and setting						
Two-year, very small	0	0	0	0	0	0
Two-year, small	0	0	0	0	0	0
Two-year, medium	0	0	0	0	0	0
Four-year, very small, primarily nonresidential	3	3	0	0	3	5
Four-year, very small, primarily residential	3	3	0	0	3	5
Four-year, very small, highly residential	20	23	2	10	18	28
Four-year, small, primarily nonresidential	3	3	0	0	3	5
Four-year, small, primarily residential	11	13	2	10	9	14
Four-year, small, highly residential	17	20	2	10	15	23
Four-year, medium, primarily nonresidential	2	2	0	0	2	3
Four-year, medium, primarily residential	15	17	10	48	5	8
Four-year, medium, highly residential	11	13	5	24	6	9
Exclusively graduate/professional	1	1	0	0	1	2
Accreditation status						
Accredited on show	77	89	57	88	20	95
Candidate	2	2	1	1	1	0
Closed	1	1	1	1	0	0
Probation	6	7	5	8	1	5
Warning	1	1	1	1	0	0

(cont.)

TABLE 6.4 Summary statistics of assessed categorical variables for analysis (*cont.*)

Variable	All institutions		Anchor institutions		Non-anchor institutions	
	Number	Percent	Number	Percent	Number	Percent
Degree of urbanization						
City: Large	27	31	11	52	16	25
City: Midsize	19	22	7	33	12	18
City: Small	10	12	0	0	10	15
Suburb: Large	6	7	0	0	6	9
Suburb: Midsize	2	2	0	0	2	3
Town: Fringe	2	2	0	0	2	3
Town: Distant	14	16	3	14	11	17
Town: Remote	1	1	0	0	1	2
Rural: Fringe	2	2	0	0	2	3
Rural: Distant	2	2	0	0	2	3
Rural: Remote	1	1	0	0	1	2

twenty-one (5%) anchor institutions. Even for the thirty-one non-anchor institutions who did spend more than 0% on research, a median allocated less than 5% of their core expenses on research, whereas the median anchor institutions allocated about 10% to this end.

5.1.3 Student Profile and Outcomes

Generally, anchor institutions had higher student enrollment than non-anchor institutions. For instance, the twelve-month enrollment for non-anchor institutions was about 2,300 students, while enrollment for the same time periods for anchor institutions was around 5,000 students. In addition, the students in anchor institutions also appeared different in terms of college preparedness. When specifically looking at institutions that did not have an open admission policy, for both math and English ACT sub scores, students at the 75th percentile of the admitted students had scores 3 points higher at anchor institutions compared to non-anchor institutions. However, it is important to note that eighteen out of the twenty-one (85%) anchor institutions reported an ACT score while only thirty-six out of the sixty-five (55%) non-anchor institutions reported an ACT score, suggesting that the percentage of anchor institutions that have an open admission policy may be lower.

Data also shows that the admissions yield between these two groups of institutions averages about 22% for both anchor and non-anchor institutions. Students at anchor institutions also seem to have continued academic outcome relative to students at non-anchor institutions, as reflected by their higher median retention rate, graduation rate, as well as lower median cohort default rate.

5.1.4 Institutional Environment

Lastly, aspects of student life also look differences between anchor and non-anchor institutions. For example, only three out of twenty-one (14%) anchor institutions are located outside of midsize to large cities, while thirty-eight out of sixty-five (58%) non-anchor institutions are located outside of midsize to large cities. Only fifty-six out of sixty-five (86%) non-anchor institutions provide an urban environment.

5.2 *Research Question 2*

Research question 2 asks: What are the "emerging" HBCUs, defined as HBCUs that do not rank in the top fifty for producing Black baccalaureate graduates who go on to earn doctorates in STEM, but have institutional characteristics that are most similar to "anchor" HBCUs, which do rank in the top fifty? To determine this, the research team devised a scoring system based on the average and standard deviation of all anchor institutions for all the variables shown in Table 6.1.[8]

Each of the eighty-six institutions in the analysis received a score of either 0, 1, or 2 for each of the twenty-five variables based on how similar they are to an average anchor institution. For instance, if the average enrollment size for all anchor institutions is 5,000 and the standard deviation is 2,000, institutions that are one (or more) standard deviation(s) below the average received a score of 0. Institutions that are within one standard deviation of the average received a score of 1 and institutions that are one (or more) standard deviation(s) above the average received a score of 2.[9]

First, measures for which a low score might inaccurately indicate better performance were "back coded." These measures were selectivity (percentage admitted), percentage Pell grant awarded, percentage awarded federal student loans, cohort default rate, and student-to-faculty ratio. Next, the amounts of 0s, 1s, and 2s were tallied for each institution to determine each institution's proximity to an average anchor institution. The score for non-anchor institutions ranged from 8 (Harris-Stowe State University) to 30 (Bowie State University). The score for anchor institutions ranged from 18 (Alabama A&M University) to 35 (Howard

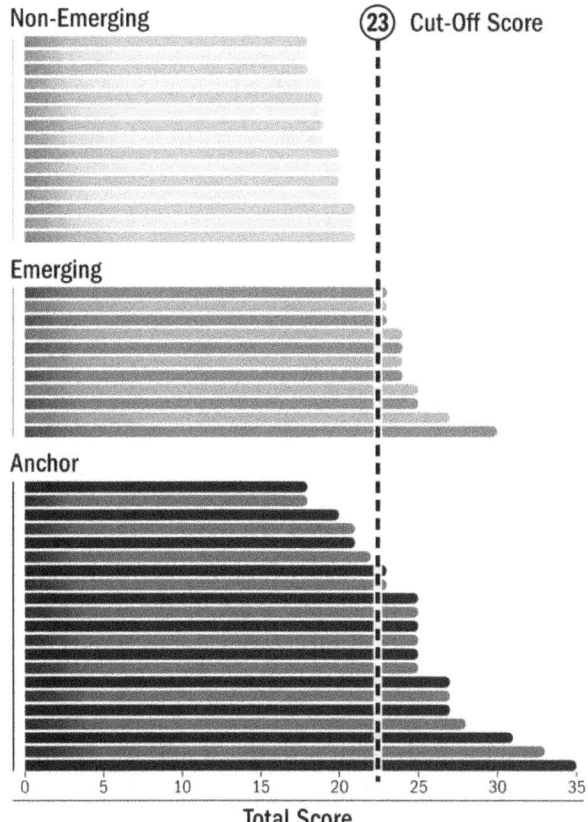

FIGURE 6.2   Anchor scoring system and cutoff score for emerging institutions

University). Then, the average score between all institutions with a score that matched the anchors (between 18 and 35) was used to identify the emerging institutions. This average score was a tallied value of 23 and was used as a cut-off value for determining the emerging institutions. Hence, *emerging institutions were defined as any non-anchor HBCUs with a score of 23* (see Figure 6.2).

After the eleven emerging institutions were identified (see Table 6.5), higher education and HBCU research experts evaluated the list to provide additional validation that the institutions identified through the process are comparable to anchor institutions.

6   Discussion

This study explored HBCUs as a pathway from secondary education to a doctorate in S&E by analyzing institutional characteristics among HBCUs that rank among the highest nationally for graduating undergraduate students who

TABLE 6.5 List of emerging institutions identified

1. Albany State University
2. Alcorn University
3. Bowie State University
4. Delaware State University
5. Fayetteville State University
6. South Carolina State University
7. Texas Southern University
8. University of Arkansas at Pine Bluff
9. University of Maryland Eastern Shore
10. Virginia State University
11. Winston-Salem State University

eventually earn an S&E doctorate. In addition, the study identified HBCUs that do not rank among the highest nationally but have institutional characteristics that are similar to top-ranking HBCUs. For this study, we analyzed archival data from the US Department of Education to develop a profile of HBCUs that successfully graduated future STEM doctorates.

The number of Black students graduating with STEM majors does not currently match the proportion of Black people in the United States. HBCUs account for only 3% of US institutions of higher learning, but 10.5% of the top fifty institutions for graduating Black undergraduates who go on to receive doctorates in STEM (NSF, 2019). The United States will require a million more STEM professionals by the end of 2025. In that regard, the study seeks to identify success factors that have aided HBCUs' performance so that other HBCUs and non-HBCUs can replicate them.

Previous analyses indicate that HBCUs collectively graduate more doctoral-bound STEM majors than predominately white institutions with large Black enrollments; however, HBCU graduation rates vary considerably. The research found that HBCUs share similar institutional characteristics that can cultivate a deeper sense of belonging and stronger cultural connections among Black students. The literature was not completely clear on whether variation in the success of HBCUs is a function of lack of knowledge transfer between institutions or because of resource differences between the higher-performing HBCUs and HBCUs with lower performance levels. Moreover, the research did not elucidate the unique student and institutional characteristics that are specifically associated with HBCUs successfully preparing and graduating STEM students.

Prior research has underscored HBCUs' success with graduating Black students in STEM but has not addressed the variability in HBCUs' graduation rates and post-baccalaureate placement. The positive unifying characteristics of HBCUs, such as students' sense of belonging and strong cultural connectedness, belies the finding that some HBCUs do not produce a high number of Black STEM students who earn doctorates compared to other HBCUs. This study fills this gap in the literature by exploring institutional characteristics (e.g., financial capabilities) that can facilitate or mitigate what has already been established as common at HBCUs conducive to the success of students (e.g., teacher-student relationship quality). Below are important findings from the study.

6.1 *Summary of Findings*

Qualitative and quantitative analyses revealed some common institutional characteristics among the twenty-one HBCUs that rank among the top fifty institutions that produce Black baccalaureate graduates who subsequently earn a doctorate in STEM disciplines (anchor). Anchor institutions had a median revenue of $160 million in 2016–2017, while non-anchor institutions had $36 million. Financial resources can help institutions provide more instructional support to students, including access to research experiences. Notably, the anchor institutions invested an average of 10% of their revenue in research, while non-anchor institutions invested between 0–5% of their revenue on research. Anchor institutions also have larger average enrollments than non-anchor institutions. This likely provides anchor institutions with more access to capital, since student tuition and fees are the primary revenue source for institutions of higher education (Bracey, 2017).

Findings also revealed that anchor institutions have higher revenue and endowment savings. Institutions with more resources are typically able to provide more student, faculty, and staff support, which can increase graduation rates. However, within the context of HBCUs, we measure these findings against the tendency to conflate monetary resources with success. For example, institutions that score highest on US News Report rankings have similar advantages over all institutions of higher education that anchor HBCUs have over emerging HBCUs (e.g., finances and selectivity). Therefore, being listed as an institution with more monetary resources should not be viewed as a value statement, which also reflects a broader critique of the Western value system.

In the context of resource disparities, it is important to note how institutions might leverage resources to graduate STEM students. Having more resources could help institutions create more opportunities for undergraduate research. Undergraduate research is important for STEM graduate education. Spelman College and Morehouse College are anchor institutions, but they are not research institutions like Howard University or Florida A&M University. None of the twenty-one institutions have the highest research Carnegie classification; however, all anchor institutions spend a portion of their core expense on research.

Anchor institutions have larger enrollments, are less likely to be open admissions, and reported higher ACT scores compared to emerging institutions. These findings have the potential to denote a value proposition, rather than a material weakness, among emerging HBCUs. Historically, HBCUs have provided options for students with traditional academic shortcomings, which likely accounts for variability between anchor and emerging institutions' success with graduating Black students who go on to graduate school for STEM. Overall, it seems the best way to help non-anchor institutions to compensate for being more open with their enrollment is to give them the funding necessary to accommodate students who require more academic support.

Our results show that more anchor institutions are in urban areas compared to non-anchor institutions. This may be because urban areas offer more resources and exposure to cultural, professional, and government institutions, indirectly leading to institutions producing more Black graduates who go on to earn post-baccalaureate degrees. The policy implications suggest that rural institutions should prioritize exposing students to opportunities beyond the institutions' city.

The study results suggest that the common characteristics among the twenty-one anchor institutions can be considered within the context of strategic plans to accommodate Black students. The literature demonstrates that HBCUs embrace practices that promote a sense of belonging among students and cultivate deeper faculty-student relationships. However, the finding of this study revealed variations among HBCU performance. The previous literature can place such variation in context. The variations in institutional characteristics can facilitate or mitigate a student's sense of belonging and optimal faculty student relationships. In other words, the factors that drive success, as already revealed in the literature, may be dependent on institutional characteristics such as financial resources, administration tenure, and faculty resources.

The study was based on institutional theory, which shows the role that institutional conformity to symbolic actions has on the formal structures of organizations. The results indicate that emerging institutions may experience normative, coercive, and mimetic isomorphism, whereby cultural expectations create an informal force for non-anchor institutions to change policies and practices. However, any changes in admission policies, instructional priorities, and resource allocation should be examined within the context of the broader institutional mission. Potential isomorphic pressures that HBCUs can face are: (1) accreditation based on racially biased assessments (coercive); (2) prioritizing research over teaching (mimetic); and (3) rigid admissions standards (normative).

6.2 *Limitations*

The study relied on secondary data that were examined retrospectively. In that case, the study has some threats to external validity, considering that the secondary data was mined from databases that collected the data for other purposes. However, developing a scoring system using the identified institutional factors helped to mitigate some limitations. The study took a snapshot approach, thus affecting the study results' reliability. A time-series study might enhance the tracking of data across a period. Another limitation of this study was the lack of student and faculty perspectives. The data used for this study was collected by university administrators and submitted to the US government. Future research on this topic should survey students and faculty members of HBCUs to understand the relationship between institutional resources and student experiences.

6.3 *Implications*

The twenty-one anchor institutions have succeeded in educating African Americans in STEM courses. The unique factors that influence their success could be replicated by non-anchor institutions so that the United States can achieve its labor market demands for STEM professionals. Such a move would increase racial equality in the workplace while improving the well-being of minorities. However, administrators and policymakers in higher institutions must make deliberate efforts to adopt strategic measures that will reinforce a sense of belonging among learners while increasing institutional revenue. Strategic measures in revenue generation, coupled with prudent use of resources, will improve HBCUs' ranking and attract donor funding. In the long-run, such steps would mean that more Black students will pursue STEM courses, proceed to pursue doctorate degrees in the same fields, and develop successful careers.

Acknowledgment

The findings are based upon work supported by the National Science Foundation under Grant No. 1760961. Any opinions, findings, and conclusions or recommendations expressed in this material are those of the authors and do not necessarily reflect the views of the NSF.

Notes

1 According to the National Science Foundation, National Center for Science and Engineering Statistics, 2019, *Women, Minorities, and Persons with Disabilities in Science and Engineering: 2019*, Special Report NSF 19-304, Alexandria, VA. Available at https://www.nsf.gov/statistics/wmpd. Of graduates who earned an S&E doctorate degree between 2013 and 2017, 25% earned a bachelor's degree from an HBCU.
2 We use "African Americans" to denote persons, or cultural experiences related to persons, of Black African ancestry who permanently reside in the United States of America. We use "Black" when referring to information that uses racial classifications to denote persons of Black African ancestry in the United States, regardless of permanent residence or cultural or ethnic affiliation.
3 At the time of the analysis, IPEDS data were available for the 2016–2017 school year. Accreditation status was available for 2018. Cohort default rate was available for 2015.
4 The following six variables were derived from the IPEDS dataset: twelve-month enrollment stability, male-to-female ratio, revenue per student, grants and contracts, percentage of faculty members with tenure, and percentage of faculty members who are African American.
5 Three variables – Carnegie size and settings, degree of urbanization, and accreditation status – were not used in the "emerging" school selection. These variables were categorical and not amenable to the scoring method used to identify the emerging institutions.
6 As indicated above, since Howard and Spellman universities were outliers in revenue and endowment numbers, they were excluded before scoring institutions on these measures to identify the emerging institutions.
7 Howard and Spelman universities were strong outliers on financial metrics such as revenue and endowment amount.
8 Three variables – Carnegie size and settings, degree of urbanization, and accreditation status – were not used in the "emerging" school selection. These variables were categorical and not amenable to the scoring method used to identify the emerging institutions.
9 As indicated previously, since Howard and Spellman universities were outliers in revenue and endowment numbers, they were excluded before scoring institution on these measures to identify the emerging institutions.

References

Adams, T., Robinson, D., Covington, A., & Talley-Matthews, S. (2017). Fueling the STEMM pipeline: How historically Black colleges and universities improve the presence of African American scholars in STEMM. *Journal of Urban Learning, Teaching, and Research*, 13, 9–25.

Brown, B. A., Mangram, C., Sun, K., Cross, K., & Raab, E. (2017). Representing racial identity: Identity, race, and the construction of the African American STEM students. *Urban Education*, 52(2), 170–206.

Carnegie Classification of Institutions of Higher Education. (2020). *Institution lookup.* https://carnegieclassifications.iu.edu/lookup/lookup.php

DiMaggio, P. J., & Powell, W. W. (1983). The iron cage revisited: Institutional isomorphism and collective rationality in organizational fields. *American Sociological Review, 48*, 63–82.

Fakayode, S. O., Yakubu, M., Adeyeye, O. M., Pollard, D. A., & Mohammed, A. K. (2014). Promoting undergraduate STEM education at a historically Black college and university through research experience. *Journal of Chemical Education, 91*(5), 662–665.

Gasman, M., & Nguyen, T. H. (2016). Engaging voices: Methods for studying STEM education at historically Black colleges and universities (HBCUs). *Journal for Multicultural Education, 10*(2), 194–205.

Government Accountability Office. (2018). *Science, technology, engineering, and mathematics education: Action needed to better assess the federal investment.* United States Government.

Graf, N., Fry, R., & Funk, C. (2018). *7 facts about the STEM workforce.* Pew Research Center. https://www.pewresearch.org/fact-tank/2018/01/09/7-facts-about-the-stem-workforce/

Hicks, T., & Wood, J. L. (2016). A meta-synthesis of academic and social characteristic studies. *Journal for Multicultural Education, 10*(2), 107–123.

Jackson, D. L. (2013). A balancing act: Impacting and initiating the success of African American female community college transfer students in STEM into the HBCU environment. *Journal of Negro Education, 82*(3), 255–271. doi:10.7709/jnegroeducation.82.3.0255

Jett, C. C. (2013). HBCUs propel African American male mathematics majors. *Journal of African American Studies, 17*(2), 189–205.

Kendricks, K., Nedunuri, K. V., & Arment, A. R. (2013). Minority student perceptions of the impact of mentoring to enhance academic performance in STEM disciplines. *Journal of STEM Education: Innovations and Research, 14*(2).

Lundy-Wagner, V. C. (2013). Is it really a man's world? Black men in science, technology, engineering, and mathematics at historically Black colleges and universities. *Journal of Negro Education, 82*(2), 157–168.

Meyer, J. W., & Rowan, B. (1977). Institutionalized organizations: Formal structure as myth and ceremony. *American Journal of Sociology, 83*(2), 340–363.

National Science Foundation. (2019). *National Science Board science & engineering indicators 2016: Characteristics of the US higher education system.* https://nsf.gov/statistics/2016/nsb20161/#/report/chapter-2

National Science Foundation, National Center for Science and Engineering Statistics. (2019). *Women, minorities, and persons with disabilities in science and engineering: 2019.* Special Report NSF 19-304. https://www.nsf.gov/statistics/wmpd

Palmer, R. T., Davis, R. J., & Thompson, T. (2010). Theory meets practice: HBCU initiatives that promote academic success among African Americans in STEM. *Journal of College Student Development, 51*, 440–443.

Perna, L., Lundy-Wagner, V., Drezner, N. D., Gasman, M., Yoon, S., Bose, E., & Gary, S. (2009). The contribution of HBCUs to the preparation of African American women for STEM careers: A case study. *Research in Higher Education, 50*(1), 1–23.

Richards, D. A. R., & Awokoya, J. T. (2012). *Understanding HBCU retention and completion.* Frederick D. Patterson Research Institute, UNCF.

Simms, K., & Bock, S. (2014). Are historically Black colleges and universities (HBCUs) in the United States a single institutional group?: Evidence from educational outcomes. *Education Research and Perspectives, 41*, 115.

Smith, D. J. (2016). Operating in the middle: The experiences of African American female transfer students in STEM degree programs at HBCUs. *Community College Journal of Research and Practice, 40*(12), 1025–1039.

Strayhorn, T. L., Williams, M. S., Tillman-Kelly, D., & Suddeth, T. (2012). Sex differences in graduate school choice for Black HBCU bachelor's degree recipients: A national analysis. *Journal of African American Studies, 17*, 174–188.

Tolbert, P. S., & Zucker, L. G. (1996). *The institutionalization of institutional theory.* Cornell University ILR School.

Toldson, I. A. (2013). Historically Black colleges and universities can promote leadership and excellence in STEM [Editor's commentary]. *Journal of Negro Education, 84*(4), 415–421.

Toldson, I. A. (2018). Why historically Black colleges and universities are successful with graduating Black baccalaureate students who subsequently earn doctorates in STEM [Editor's commentary]. *Journal of Negro Education, 87*(2), 95–98. doi:10.7709/jnegroeducation.87.2.0095

Toldson, I. A. (2019). *No BS (bad stats): Black people need people who believe in Black people enough not to believe every bad thing they hear about Black people.* Brill Sense.

Toldson, I. A., & Esters, L. L. (2012). *The quest for excellence: Supporting the academic success of minority males in science, technology, engineering, and mathematics (STEM) disciplines.* Association of Public and Land-grant Universities.

United States Census Bureau. (2018). *Quick facts.* https://www.census.gov/quickfacts/fact/table/US/PST045218

US Bureau of Labor Statistics. (2015). *Monthly labor review: STEM crisis or STEM surplus? Yes and yes.* https://www.bls.gov/opub/mlr/2015/article/stem-crisis-or-stem-surplus-yes-and-yes.htm

US Department of Education. (2016). *Fact sheet: Spurring African-American STEM degree completion.* https://www.ed.gov/news/press-releases/fact-sheet-spurring-african-american-stem-degree-completion

www.ingramcontent.com/pod-product-compliance
Lightning Source LLC
Chambersburg PA
CBHW061958220426
43662CB00011B/1732